PRAYERS
OF FAITH

On Learning to Trust God

Faith Annette Sand

HOPE PUBLISHING HOUSE
Pasadena, California

Prayers of Faith

For information address:
    Hope Publishing House
    P.O. Box 60008
    Pasadena, CA 91116
    Phone: 818-792-6123, Fax: 818-792-2121

Design and composition by Greg Endries
Cover detail from seventeenth-century Russian icon

Printed in the U.S.A. on acid-free paper

Library of Congress Cataloging-in-Publication Data

Sand, Faith Annette, 1939-
    Prayers of faith : on learning to trust God / Faith Annette Sand.
        p. cm.
    ISBN 0-932727-79-4 (alk. paper). — ISBN 0-932727-78-6 (pbk. :
alk. paper)
    1. Sand, Faith Annette, 1939-   2. Anglicans—United States—
Biography 3. Missionaries—Brazil—Biography. 4. Missionaries—
United States—Biography 5. Christian literature—Publication and
distribution—United States—Biography 6. Prayer—Christianity
    I. Title.
    BX5995.S24A3 1996
    283'.092—dc20
    [B]   95-47070
                                                                   CIP

*Dedicated to the women who have cared for me,
nurtured me and guided me on
my pilgrimage of prayer:*

Addie, Ana, Maruja, Borghild, Helen,
Gudrun, Freda, Agnes, Edith,
Alice and Margie

CONTENTS

PROLOGUE

It was the Pilgrim's costume that started me on my prayer life. I was seven that cold, blustery day when I found you could ask God for a miracle and get what you prayed for. Our family was recently back in Minneapolis after having lived in the tropics for three years, and I had just come down with measles. Today the episode seems more like "trivial pursuits," but at the time it was momentous. All I knew was that God had healed me miraculously so I could wear the Pilgrim's costume. From this tiny mustard seed experience grew a confidence that when all is said and done, God is the only One who is always there for you.

This incredible answer to my childish plea lodged at the base of my being. From that day forward none of the other tribulations of my life could shake that rock-solid confidence that a God who was willing to intervene in a three-day measles episode so I could wear the Pilgrim's colonial costume in the Thanksgiving assembly at school must love me beyond anything that I could logically understand.

It began the morning our teacher stood us all up around the room. This was my first exposure to the American school system and I was trying to fit in, but it did seem, for reasons not made too clear, you spent an inordinate amount of time forming straight lines. It turned out the aim of this current lineup was the teacher's desire to size us by height. Happily I was the smallest girl in the class which meant I was chosen to wear the Pilgrim costume at the PTA Thanksgiving program. Years before, some enterprising benefactor had stitched together a girl's and a boy's Pilgrim costume for the class. By now, the third grade had been responsible for the Pilgrim parts in the program for a long time. However, over the years, third graders had grown larger thanks to all the fresh milk, fruits and vegetables added to the American diet. Our teacher certainly did not want the Piligrim roles to go to her second-grade rival, so she was obliged to squeeze the smallest girl and boy from the class into the costumes.

My being the smallest and the youngest in the class—and thus eligible for the costume—was mostly due to a fluke. During the three years we had been in Colombia, South America, where my parents served as Lutheran missionaries, I had meandered through a rather infelicitous school career (it turned out to be the beginning of a wretched habit I was never able to break). Children on the mission field were to be seen and not heard, of course, but since their presence interfered with the Lord's real work getting done, they were mostly shunted to whatever would least hinder those dedicated endeavors.

A few days after arriving in Medellín, Colombia, my parents were to start language school. Since they didn't know what to do with a four-year-old while they were in classes all day long, they decided to send me to a "native" school—which would keep me from being underfoot most of the day. It was a rather miserable solution. Not only was I too young for the school, but I understood nothing communicated. I was to learn Spanish quickly, but not soon enough to keep me from getting in trouble the first day I went to school. Nor could I fathom why I was being punished.

Medellín has one of the world's best climates—it sits in an Andean bowl at 5,000 feet near the equator, so it never gets above 80° nor below 64°. All the classrooms were airy, having merely three walls. The fourth side opened on a courtyard because the only natural element you needed protection from was the warm tropical rain that fell most afternoons. More serious protection was necessary to safeguard you from unnatural elements—thus the enclosed, interior patios with inlaid broken glass shards marching along the outside perimeters—sentinels dissuading would-be intruders. This design freely allowed in the breezes perfumed with myriad tropical flowers. With this basic fort-mentality, homes and establishments bolstered themselves against all comers behind solid walls facing the street with only tiny, iron-grilled windows to let you see out a bit.

I found myself being dressed in a stiff, uncomfortable uniform—navy skirt with suspenders and a scratch-starched white shirt—to attend this severely regimented school. That first day, sitting in my four-year-old wonder, perplexed and language-dumb, trying to ape my peers in strange quarters, I scrambed to follow the lead of those around me. Suddenly the class erupted up on their seats to check out a roaring novelty. Over the school's courtyard swooped a squadron of American planes. This was 1943 and World War II was in full force. Some Allied bureaucrat had just decided that Medellín would be a perfect spot for R&R and the first contingent of vacationing troops were arriving.

For leaping up on my chair to get a better view of the flyby I was not allowed to have a recess from my allotted bench but had to sit it out while the lucky few who had kept their seats went to play. Our cook's niece was assigned the task of walking me to and from school. As soon as we got home, word of my misconduct was out. My parents tried to explain why I was not supposed to stand on my chair, but I was disconsolate. Even at that young age I had a well-honed sense of justice and knew that I shouldn't be punished for actions I did not know were beyond the limits.

So persistent was my resistance to returning to this school that finally a single Lutheran missionary, who happened to be living with us while she and my parents were learning Castilian at the local language school for missionaries, took pity and offered to administer a Calvert correspondence course when it fit into her study schedules. I don't think Addie was necessarily a born teacher, but I adored her and the course was rather self-explanatory. There wasn't much going on in my life, so I quickly zoomed along.

The next three years I kept chugging away at my studies, happy in my solitary world. Perhaps it was the indolent setting, but no one noticed that I had probably advanced too quickly with my school work until we came back to the U.S. on emergency medical leave just a few days after my seventh birthday. It was May, so school was winding down for the year, but better in the classroom than underfoot. As soon as we hit Minneapolis I was duly enrolled in the school nearest the mission headquarters where we were staying.

The administrator accepting me into the system didn't have time to test me and so decided that I could start out in the second grade classroom where I would be going in the fall. This way the teacher could ascertain my level to see if I would fit in her class come September. It didn't take long to demonstrate that my correspondence course had given me skills yet to come for the rest of her class about to graduate to the third grade. Not hankering a know-it-all under her tutelage for a full year, she bundled me off with the rest of the lot when June came.

Regardless of how I tried to blend in, I knew I was different. Instead of living with my family in a nice house with a white picket fence, we were the ones living with all those other people in a huge brick mansion which had fallen on hard times when the war effort disappeared the serving class. It had stood empty and forlorn until finally it was sold for a pittance to our mission for a headquarters to house missionary families preparing to go or return from the mission field. (I gradually discovered it did have its good features such as the turntable floor in the garage designed to facilitate parking a stable of Model-As but which served as a great merry-go-round when you put one foot on the turntable and pushed on the floor with the other one until you'd gotten yourself into a spin. And there was the dumbwaiter that went up the middle of the house which I never had the courage to use as a small elevator, but which would courier objects up and down if there were no adults around to discourage your play.) But at school it was the sidelines where I normally stood, watching the others at play.

Life suddenly brightened when the Pilgrim part appeared. Thanksgiving was an unremembered holiday and the Pilgrims' story still a bit vague, but the outfit was superb. After that decisive lineup from which I emerged the chosen one, the teacher led me into the cloakroom to try on a delightfully swishy long black skirt, a hand-embroidered white pinafore and a black-and-white cap contraption that perched on my flaxen head. From being the timid onlooker, I became the center of attention. My longed-for triumphal entry approached. Rehearsals were over. Parts memorized.

Then on the Monday before Thanksgiving I woke with red spots all over my body. Mother, a nurse, nodded sagely and proclaimed, "Three-day measles."

When the full implication of that statement was explained to me, I was disconsolate. How could I be confined for three days and miss the school program scheduled for Wednesday? It was a tragedy too heavy for my tiny soul. Finally, responding to my anguish, Mother suggested we pray and ask Jesus to heal me so I could go back to school the next day. I put all my faith into that short prayer and pled with God to foreshorten my bout with this malady.

And that's what happened. God heard my prayer. My measles disappeared that afternoon. Mother hoped I wasn't contagious, but didn't have the effrontery to suggest I remain in bed after she herself had prayed for my miraculous healing.

This was a small beginning to a life of prayer, but never again could I doubt that the God who loved me enough to heal me of this trifling ailment—so I could participate in an inconsequential event—was worthy of my trust. I also knew that this God who had listened to my childish plea had set up a relationship with me that absolutely no one could impugn. Afterward when I came across doubters or even was around believers who felt that I wasn't good enough to be worthy of God's attention—or that God had too much to handle to be bothered with my petty afflictions—I knew better. I would nod agreeably and say, "I understand why you feel that way but I just really believe in prayer."

That simple request, engendered by my childish distress, started me on a life of learning to trust God that has carried me around the world. Along the way I have developed many axioms on prayer—the central one being that there are no "rules" that work. God is much too great to be boxed into a system or structure that would require that whenever I prayed for "A" God would be obliged to produce "B". In some ways it seems almost a contradiction in terms to attempt writing a book on prayer. Every day I wake up wondering what's it all about. Why does the God of the universe deign to answer my prayers? I can't figure it out. Yet each day I bring to God my joys and my sorrows, my hurts and my longings and know beyond a shadow that time and again God supernaturally intervenes in my life. Daily I see that God provides, protects and prods me along my journey of faith.

What did I do to deserve this? Nothing! Maybe that's the secret. No one ever had to convince me how absurd it was to think that the Creator of the universe bothered to be involved in my life. Yet I know this is true. Later when the vagaries of life dropped eight adopted children and then two of my own into my life, I was given countless opportunities to learn what prayer could mean when confronting problems of life which at the time seemed overwhelming.

Because prayer was becoming such a foundation to my existence, I then found myself gravitating to others who moved in the world of prayer. From these encounters and experiences down through the years, I have garnered many postulates on how God deals with us on this pilgrimage of learning to trust the Lord. As one friend quoted when I tried to explain how presumptuous it seemed for me to undertake such a project as writing a book on prayer, "Just think of it as one poor beggar telling another beggar where to find bread."

On that note I decided to jot down a few principles that I have gleaned over the years through my association with some wonderful

guides from every corner of the globe. I haven't always accepted everything they tried to teach me, but I have used those tenets that function
for me and developed others that I learned. This is an experiential
reflection—based on what I've found to work as well as the basic
premises which I feel underlie them. Prayer for me has always been an
avenue to wonderful adventure. A motivating factor for sharing these
thoughts is the hope that they will prove useful to others on their own
pilgrimage of faith, opening doors on the great exploits awaiting all
who relate to the Creator of all that is, seen and unseen.

Often what I have asked for has been denied by God. Some denials
are harder to take than others. But all my prayers have been heard.
Inexplicably I know this and so the daily dialogue continues. As a
mother, it makes perfect sense. Just as we don't (or shouldn't) give our
own children everything they ask for, so God sometimes rejects our
petitions. Learning to say "please" and "thank you" is one of the first
lessons we teach our children and basically that's where God starts
with us as well. As we have to teach our children the skill of listening
and paying attention, so too does God.

At times the "still, small voice" is distinct. Not always is it rational
or even reasonable—then it is easy to ignore the voice, but most of
the time we discover later that to do so is at our own peril. "Discernment" is the established term for this skill. Raising many children has
helped me become a more intuitive person because much of mother-
hood consists in responding to the unarticulated needs of our children. It is at the intuitive level that you begin this conversation with
God. What does this situation mean? What is the Lord trying to say
to me out of these circumstances?

It surprises me to find that some people shy away from prayer as
being an almost disrespectful act—as if they shouldn't bother God
with their own picayune problems. They seem to have a grading system for prayer requests. I have noted these same people tend to perceive grievous afflictions as exempt from this proscription, so when a
child lies at death's door with leukemia or a hurricane is about to blast

a community off the face, then such troubles can be taken to the Lord in prayer—especially by a religious "professional" who is regarded as trained and disciplined in prayer and able to access God. Lesser difficulties and trials are to be borne stoically without complaining or disturbing God overmuch.

Yet I simply will not concede there are minimum-pain thresholds that must be reached before you take a matter to the Lord in prayer. Or that a level of spiritual training must be achieved before God's ear is turned your way. There are no secret, Delphic mysteries to the prayer life. Everyone has the same route to God. Christ came to earth to tell us all, "I am the way." The corollary to this wonderful news was the message Jesus left his followers, "Go tell everyone that the Kingdom of God is at hand."

Thus the good news of the Gospel is that a life of prayer is for all of us, regardless of where we are on our pilgrim journey of faith. I believe the Lord answers everyone's prayers because God is no respecter of persons. The trivial pursuits which mattered to me as a seven-year-old were no less important to God than the life-necessities which mattered to me as a 30-year-old trying to provide food and clothing for my ten children in a very primitive setting on the mission field. Don't ask me why—it makes no sense—but I know God caught my attention by answering my prayer when I was seven. From that day on I knew I could bring my concerns to God and expect them to be taken seriously by the Creator of the universe. Granted, when you consider the vastness of the universe it seems a bit out of proportion, but we're not talking rationality. The issue is a communication system set up with the supernatural, transcendent Lord of all the earth.

I have found that my prayer request does not even have to appear consequential. God cares about it because God cares about me. God is willing to intervene on your behalf because God loves you more than anyone could ask or think. The only thing necessary to set up a meaningful prayer life with God is to start. Ask the Lord to help you. To intervene. Let your requests be made known unto the Lord—it's scriptural—and the Lord will bring it to pass. Once you've started on this grand adventure of trusting the Lord and bringing to God your requests, you'll never turn back because being in this kind of a relationship with the Lord is beyond anything we can ask or think.

PRAYER OF BEGINNINGS

Glorious Creator, you have started us on this earthly journey for reasons we can never comprehend. Often we are blissfully unaware of so much we have received from you—our health and strength, our shelter and protection, our sustenance and provision. May your Spirit nurture ours so that we might grow in truth to serve you in ways that are pleasing in your sight. Make us mindful of your presence whenever we face need or distress. As your unworthy servants, we come boldly asking that we might again receive, expecting anew to see the evidence of your loving attention to us. We praise you and bless you for all the times that we perceive your bountiful intervention in our lives. Give us truly thankful hearts and grant that we may learn to trust you a bit more each day. Make us worthy to be called your servants, through Christ our Lord. Amen.

1.

God's Mercy

I will sing of the mercies of the Lord forever.
I will sing . . .

Every flower that blooms, every raindrop that falls, every breath of fresh mountain air, every sun sinking into the ocean's horizon, every child's sweet gaze, every lover's cherished touch, every day of health and strength and every hint that guardian angels surround us with protective wings—all these assure us that our lives are filled with God's mercies at a level that is beyond our most exaggerated imaginations. It is my conviction that the cornerstone to a life of prayer must be a clear understanding of God's mercy, for it is the Lord's mercy which explains why God would even stoop to give us an audience when we come with our requests. Certainly, whatever response we get to our prayers is generated by the Lord's mercy.

The Psalmist tells us that God's mercies are new every morning, but we would probably be paralyzed if we had an inkling of how merciful God is to us in a host of ways past finding out. Our childish prayers that we mumbled as we went off to dreamland as well as our most informed and theologically correct adult invocations echo the Psalmist's oft-repeated plea for God's merciful intervention in all our undertakings. Basically we want our lives kept under God's mercy and we trust this same mercy will remain with us in the life to come. Amen.

Such sentiments are not unique for those who hold the Psalms as canon. A few years back I was in Chicago attending the centennial celebration of the Parliament of the World's Religions. Religious leaders from around the globe gathered at the historic Palmer House to speak (and a few to listen) to one another. There were robes of every hue and persuasions of every cast wandering the halls.

I stayed with an old friend in the Chicago suburb where I had graduated from college. Driving back and forth from this shady, manicured town which I knew so well to the parliament's venue in the middle of a jumble of roaring El trains and constipated streets gave me time to compare the rigid and puritanical world I had grown up in with the free-spirited souls who were beating drums, burning incense and dancing in the corridors of the Palmer House. It gave me pause to put the dour and judgmental looks I remembered vividly from student days at my fervently religious college in juxtaposition with the smiling, peaceful faces of those religious leaders at the parliament. Their understandings of God would make them unacceptable as students, let alone speakers, at my alma mater.

My college town is still proud to be a dry city—so if Jesus were to come back and eat with his winebibber friends, I can assure you the party would be held outside the city limits. Fence-building is a major undertaking for this academic community because at all costs you must keep out the infidel. The school's motto, "For Christ and His Kingdom," has always meant that strangers need not apply. Even though the school was founded by renowned abolitionists, my class graduating a hundred years later had only a few token minority members admitted. The situation is a little better now, but not much.

If mercy was a major concern anywhere in this college community, or in any of the other Christian schools I was bundled off to, it never got communicated to me. I remember a lot of laws and guilt and fear and judgments. And a lot of sermon illustrations—examples of what you should *not* do or be because of the ruination that came to those feckless who did or were. In order to register for college classes we had first to pledge ourselves to abstain from alcohol, tobacco, movies, dances and playing cards. A decade later during all the campus unrest in this country these pledges were modified when cheeky protestors pointed out that you could fornicate, assassinate and prevaricate and keep the pledge, but late night movies on TV were still taboo.

What I remember best from all the Christian schools I was sent to was the huge list of things that the school administration assured us made God unhappy. Our opinions were not asked, wanted or listen-ed to, and we quickly learned that to question why some rule was imposed brought us a sermon on the sins of murmuring and a des-cription of the wrath of God that descended on those with a rebel-lious attitude. Of course, the girls' list of no-noes was always longer than the boys'. We couldn't wear Bermuda shorts, they could. We couldn't ride motorcycles, they could. We had an earlier curfew, and no one even thought about asking for equal sports opportunities. After my eight years in Christian boarding schools, the impression deeply imbedded was that making—and breaking—rules was the primary focus of our religious experience in these so-called bastions of Christian education.

Even in those days it was hard for me to lay all this pettiness on God. It never crossed my mind to wonder if God cared whether we wore Bermudas under our trench coats until we were out of sight. Nor did it seem of weighty theological import when we tweaked Prexy's beak by anonymously sending his wife Bermudas for her birthday. Sure, God wanted us to be obedient to civil authorities, but when did the school administration ever show itself to be civil?

Deep down I knew that the God who related to me and who was revealed through scripture seemed more concerned about the blind seeing, the lame walking and the imprisoned being freed than in all the rules being observed. It was in the footsteps of the Pharisees that the school administrators were walking. They were offended when their Sabbath rules were broken. They were rigid in applying their standards to one and all—regardless of the circumstances. And money and accumulating "stuff" meant more to them than caring for feeble relatives, feeding their neighbors or helping the poor survive.

When I graduated from college I had been carefully taught: justice was the issue, not mercy; being upright was more important than being compassionate; the appearance of evil was to be avoided at all costs because that is what got the neighbors to talking and the trustees to balking at granting more bequests. So my crowd slipped away from the church and its institutions, because the love of Christ was buried beneath a façade of rightness. It was all F.C. (fundamentally correct) but calamitous to our spiritual health.

On leaving those hallowed halls of ivy, I didn't exactly discount all the sermonizers, but close—especially those who were downright angry, mean people who seemed to pull on their sanctimonious robes of rightness as they provoked to anger those who dared disagree. So much was just pure power struggle. I was tempted to wonder whether any of them might be woefully surprised to hear Christ's reproach: "Depart from me, I never knew you," when the roll is called up yonder.

Although decades had passed since I had left, being back in the Chicago area made all these memories whirl. Why, I asked myself, was I so attracted to these religious leaders whose beliefs were at variance with my own that I hoped those of congruous doctrine would not cross the paths of these visiting clerics and give Christianity a bad name in the process? Or at least I hoped God was into damage control enough that should they come upon one another, my co-religionists wouldn't be a total embarrassment with their unattractive and really superficial expressions of the Christian faith we share.

In spite of my uneasiness at how my conservative world communicates its faith, when someone at the Palmer House commented that this interfaith meeting proved how all religions have so much in common, I disagreed. Not according to my reading of the Gospel! Certainly it is normative for all religions to teach their adherents those incantations and prayers which allow them to ask (or demand) from God mercies on themselves and their own—family, loved ones and those who deserve kind treatment. But Christ laid on his followers a totally revolutionary precept when he explained that those who would be his followers had a different criterion for pleading for God's mercies.

A basic tenet of the Christian faith, Jesus carefully and consistently taught, is that his followers are to ask God's blessings on their enemies, on those who despitefully use them, and on those who want to do them harm—the mean and the nasties. (When I finally realized how important it is for our Christian pilgrimage to learn this lesson of being merciful as Christ is merciful, it finally made sense why God had allowed all those obnoxious souls into my life! I was graciously being given ample opportunity to show my mettle with evidence there was slight justification for calling myself by Christ's name.)

To prove how serious he was about this injunction, Jesus modeled this kind of behavior under the most gruesome conditions. Hanging on the cross, dying a hideous and painful death occasioned by evil and ruthless persons who were afraid Jesus was a threat to their religious power-base, this innocent person with an impressive track record and an obviously vital prayer life, managed to plead their case: "Father, forgive them."

The paragon of our faith demonstrated the appropriate Christian response: Have mercy upon my enemies. In his agony, thinking of these vile people who had made this preëmptive move against him, Christ begged that compassion be shown them, magnanimously pointing out their ignorance: "they know not what they do." No vengeance. No justice. Not even a request for alleviation of his own pain. Just a plea for mercy for those who were too blinded by their ambition to comprehend what they were doing. Even the Psalmist never asked for such mercy. Rather it was: Help me escape from those who would brutalize me. Wreak vengeance on those who would harm me. Provide for me and mine. Show me your mercies which are new every morning, but in the meantime, smash my enemies to smithereens.

Jesus, on the other hand, instituted a unique, innovative covenant—a New Testament. As followers of Christ—however feeble and ineffectual—we are told that, unfortunately, we have no choice in the matter. Simply put, we are to love our enemies. The criterion for judging whether or not the Holy Spirit has been able to move in our hearts and produce even a modicum of spiritual conversion will be based on our ability not just to forgive our enemies but to do good to them. We must go the second mile when they demand only one, turn the other cheek while the other one is still stinging. When someone tries to cheat us out of a jacket, we are to give them an overcoat as well. And then if that isn't enough, we are then to ask their forgiveness for judging them (as thieves, cheats and bullies) and come to God on their behalf saying, "Have mercy. There but for your grace go I." No death-penalty advocates can find exoneration in the last sayings of Christ from the cross.

No wonder so many in Christendom spend their energies on obeying rules and keeping up façades rather than digging into the content of the Gospel. The demands that Christ makes of his followers are onerous. It never gets any easier, it would seem. But the amazing thing is to realize that Christ exacts this of his followers in order to free us from our slavery.

We are free at last from whining materialism when we don't have to protect our property and empire from all comers. We are liberated from the suffocating tentacles of our pride when we are willing to be overlooked, demeaned and insulted—and can be happy with the worst seat on the bus. Our enemies no longer control or dominate us through our strangulating hatred when we can look on them in compassion and understanding instead of loathing them and promising revenge. My head tells me that if I were truly a follower of Christ I would want to give a generous tip to the waiter who has just provided demeaning service and overcharged us. Instead my impulse is to berate his arrogant idiocy and complain to the manager.

The times are few and far between when I have been able to channel God's love to my enemies. But those rare experiences have been powerfully emancipating and rewarding. (I admit that I've yet to pull it off with a cheating or incompetent clerk.) Yet this is the one promise Christ made that is almost impossible to practice—"Judge not that ye be not judged."

In the beginning I used to think that if I were good enough, God would reward me with happiness and joy and blessings on every hand. Then I figured out that my God who was worthy of my trust was willing to give me what I asked for, not because I deserved it but because of the truth that we have a loving God who is willing to do good things for us, God's children, just because we say "please"—and hopefully, "thank you." Since my repute has never come from the "Being Good" side of the ledger, it used to irritate some when God showered me with mercy anyhow. How come I got to go on all those adventures? Whenever I explained that I had prayed and asked God for it specifically so my latest junket was a direct answer to prayer, the Goody-Two-Shoes around me had apoplectic fits.

In all this, I do not mean to imply that I did not take God's laws seriously. If it was in the Bible, I accepted it as my mandate. I just couldn't always pull it off—or hide my irritation. Turning the other cheek or letting someone cheat me without complaining is not my best attribute. Of course I realize that if I had the mind of Christ in me, I would be able to do this, but as yet I'm still stumbling along my pilgrimage journey, sailing over a few rocks but tripping on others.

It finally dawned on me why the Lord was so good to me—I was being shown some important truths about God's kingdom. From the beginning of his ministry and the Sermon on the Mount to the last breath he drew on the cross, Christ proclaimed that instead of worrying about justice (and its corollary—doing the right thing), rather we should pray for those who despitefully use us (in other words throw justice to the wind and beg for mercy for the offenders). In the process of doing all this, we would begin to fathom a little of how God treats us—for after all, in God's sight all our righteousness appears as so many filthy rags. In the Sermon on the Mount, Jesus announces that by loving our enemies we "will be the true children of God in heaven" who "is good even to people who are unthankful and cruel" (Lk 6:35).

Which explains the great truth I somehow blundered on: instead of being so good that God would feel obligated to be nice to me—a maxim under which a lot of people around me seemed to operate—I could come and ask the Lord who "is good even to people who are unthankful and cruel" to please help me with some problem or give me some desire of my heart or help me find something I'd lost. When this happened, I made sure I didn't fall into the unthankful category and gave God the credit. Extrapolating these insights to their logical conclusions, it appears the goal of our prayer life is not that we achieve a placid and comfortable life surrounded by luxury and ease—and fairness. Rather, with all the escapades and answers to prayer that I was receiving, I finally figured it out: God was just trying to get my attention.

Jesus explained it to those at the Mount: "Anyone who comes and *listens* to me and *obeys* me is like someone who dug down deep and built a house on solid rock" (Lk 6:47-48). Then when the storms of life pommeled those who have built on solid rock, they would stand firmly rooted. When your foundations are rock solid, the nasties around can lash out, but you can turn a nonviolent cheek and sing, "Free at last."

I came to realize that to be serious about prayer and our faith meant I was to acknowledge that the end product we are to look for is a supernatural ability to love our enemies. Thus Jesus said, "This is the way everyone will know that you are my disciples—that you love one another. That you love your enemies. That you pray for those that persecute you."

Of course! Without the supernatural intervention by the Holy Spirit picking us up by the scruff of the neck and saying, "Capitulate!" there isn't the slightest possibility that we Christians—Protestant, Fundamentalist, Evangelical, Orthodox or Catholic—could possibly love our neighbor, turn the other cheek or pray for them that spitefully use us. When we finally manage to do any of this, it proves to everyone around that we are under the Spirit's aegis. Obviously at this point we are marching to a strange drummer if we can let someone cheat us without having a tantrum.

In my lifetime I have listened to an inordinate number of sermons. At age 13, in the ninth grade and still underfoot, I was sent off to a remote Canadian Christian boarding school so my parents would again be freed to do "the Lord's work" unencumbered on the mission field. Boarding school was not the perfect venue for me—I did fine academically, but the deportment grades kept sliding until at the end of the year everyone agreed that I would do better elsewhere. By the time I was 16 and graduating, I'd been to three Christian high schools. I finished second in my class academically but wasn't allowed the salutatorian role for reasons the school never explained. When you are doing God's work, I've found, you don't have to justify your fiats.

All these schools felt that to nurture us in our faith, we had to attend chapel each morning, vespers in the evening and lots of services on the weekend. By the time I'd finished college I had been subjected to thousands of sermons. Even on school holidays I was in a world which expected me to attend church twice on Sunday, once in the middle of the week and at least one other time for a special evangelical presentation. I didn't always pay the closest attention, but I did hear a multitude of preachers expound on the various Gospel texts that touch on the issue of loving your enemies. Yet it was always clear that "enemies" was really a rather qualified category. Not necessarily articulated, many preachers implied this mandate did not apply (in the beginning) to the Germans, the Japanese, the Soviets or the Marxists, (or even to most) Indians, Blacks, or Catholics, (and later) it excluded the Liberals, the foreigners, the Liberation Theologians, the Contras, the Mafia, the hippies, the rock singers, the illegal immigrants, the abortion doctors and whoever else was beyond the pale. These it was okay to hate, if not murder or annihilate.

By inference, my fundamentalist world taught that the demand of Christ regarding enemies meant that if you weren't trying to blow them to Kingdom come, you might possibly get away with praying for these sinners. But it was out of the question you would ever eat with them, admit them to your schools or hospitals, or do anything other than preach at them about their need to follow Christ and be baptized by the same method that you were. It also meant that you could imprison conscientious objectors because any red-blooded American knew that God had given us this country to protect from all enemies so somewhere there was a Gospel caveat implied that allowed you to jail those who refused to take up arms and kill the nation's enemies. Even in peacetime when the country had made no official declaration of war (and somehow our "nation under God" motto means Congressional acts can supersede what Christ taught) there were circumstances that justified mayhem, bloodshed and the death penalty.

Once a conservative mission operation sent me a bulletin that pictured a graduate from my college whom I had known standing smugly in front of an army helicopter high in the Guatemalan highlands. He had been flown in by powerful friends to inspect a "pacified" Indian village. In the accompanying article, this well-known mission leader justified the wholesale massacre of hundreds of villagers who were "Communists." (Children are apparently born ideologically indoctrinated in those parts.) He concluded with an appeal to the American Fundamentalist community to give generously and support a "Guns and Beans" project to help arm and feed the troops under Guatemala's beleaguered president, Rios Montt, cited as the first Protestant president of that cheerless nation.

Having just been to Guatemala on a consulting job I was appalled. The article failed to tell you that in Guatemala this so-called "Believer" president was called "General Butcher" for his bloodthirsty approach towards ridding the country of the restless. High on the slopes of the quiescent volcanoes that dot that land, I had met Indian women who eked out a living from their serf-like existence. They introduced me to their children (in shabby but clean homespun clothes) who shyly approached this *estrangeira* to greet me in proper Guatemalan fashion. These mothers wanted for their children what I wanted for mine—a decent life, a chance to be educated and an opportunity to grow up and be a credit to their family and their community.

It didn't take long to learn that their woes were legion. The school-teacher assigned to their village appeared only sporadically because he was a relative of a some government official and so was paid whether or not he taught. The mothers had tried to complain through chan-nels, but it was made clear to them that to do so was to invite disas-trous recriminations. Their land belonged to others and they received only a small percentage of the harvest from the tired soil where they scrimped out a living. When I asked if they could ever hope to buy their own fields, they shook their heads sadly. Earning the pittance they were paid for their labor in this vassal-style existence made it unthinkable for them to amass the necessary fortune it would require to buy the tiniest plot of farmland.

The crime for which their Guatemalan neighbors were killed and which my fellow alumnus was defending was that they lived on tradi-tional tribal land that turned out to be mineral-rich and thus was cov-eted by someone in power. By calling these indigenous people who claimed ancestral rights to the land "rebel-sympathizers" or "Com-munists" and killing all those who refused to be scared off the land and relocated in "safe" villages or refugee camps, the authorities could make the land "safe for democracy"—and free to be expropriated by one of Rios Montt's brigands.

At least my gun-fostering fellow-alumnus had the grace to look embarrassed and mutter something inconsequential when I asked him years later at an alumni gathering how he could possibly justify championing the distribution of guns as a means of evangelism. Unfortunately he was a typical product of the rigid, fundamentalist Christian world that spawned us. No one ever shoved that verse about loving your enemies down our throats—and they modeled this even less. We were carefully taught by example that our world was best. Lamentably, our Christian education wasn't shabby in training us to feel righteous and holier-than-thou. The basic assumption was that since we eschewed worldly pleasures and went to church all the time we were virtually worthy of God's love and mercy.

Even though I grew up surrounded by Christians, the issue pounded into us was justice, not mercy. When Christian leaders gathered around our family's dining room table, the conversations and small talk you heard tended to revert to who had wronged whom, who was caught in sin, why injustice prevailed and what could be done to bring about restitution.

Only gradually over the years did it begin to sink in that this preoccupation with justice wasn't quite scriptural. I kept getting hints along the way that there was more grace abounding than I or anyone else deserved. Several times in my pilgrimage I observed God mercifully stepping in to keep me from becoming another sermon illustration—even when there were those ready to take up battle stations and call down fire and brimstone on my head when I questioned their authority. Finally, years later, the light went on when I was invited to a Catholic retreat.

In days gone by this would have seemed like consorting with the enemy, but this was the '80s and we tended to be more sophisticated and cosmopolitan in our maturity. Thus I found myself quietly listening to a riveting exposition on God's mercy followed by a slow reading of Matthew's rendition of the Sermon on the Mount (ch. 5-7). This, the lay leader explained, is what we are called to obey (there were no Dispensationalists in the crowd to lop those chapters off the canon that applies to our era). We were then instructed by the retreat leaders to go silently and find a quiet corner to reread this passage prayerfully and spend 30 minutes on our knees saying the Jesus Prayer.

I had already published a book on the Jesus Prayer (*The Way of a Pilgrim*) and loved the simple profundity of both the shorter version, "Lord Jesus, have mercy on me," and the longer one, "Lord Jesus Christ, Son of God, have mercy on me a sinner." Even though I found it to be an inspiring prayer, I had no inkling how God's Spirit was about to move in on my territory. I went to the room I was sharing with a self-absorbed child of 30 who thought the instructions to maintain silence during this retreat were for the others. Since it kept her from talking about her favorite person, it certainly did not apply. Not realizing that I was a good Protestant rule-keeper with no easy confession/easy indulgence in my background, the first night she had merrily ignored the rule of silence and told me all her problems, chatting aimlessly while I nodded, hoping the other retreaters would not overhear and think it was I not following orders.

Shortly after going to our room to begin this new assignment, I heard the door opening and realized my roommate was headed in. In order to avoid a repeat of the past evening, I immediately fell to my knees to start the prayer cycle before my loquacious companion began another installment of her life's trials. After a few minutes of silence had passed while I remained motionless in my pietistic stance, she finally left the room to find her own sedate corner—or a more cooperative audience. Just to make sure, I remained on my knees, silently repeating the Jesus prayer.

In spite of my judgments and irritations and exasperations, suddenly in the middle of this hastily-begun exercise, I was swept with one of those gifted moments C.S. Lewis says you must appreciate when they come but never seek or try to recreate. Praying for God's mercy, I was suddenly overwhelmed by the realization that I had been receiving mercy from God in abundance throughout my life. Furthermore, it struck me that all my trials and tribulations down through the years had been the product of my own pride. My ego had produced the shackles that had enslaved me. I had tried to maintain a façade of goodness and righteousness, but instead of being swept into God's kingdom I had been sucked into a brier patch of problems and difficulties and sorrows.

Twenty years before I would never have married my abusive husband if it had not been for my pride. I had been compromised and I couldn't bear to let anyone know this, so it seemed as though I had no choice but to go ahead and marry George. He knew enough not to be violent before the wedding, but it only took days afterwards for his temper to explode. The following morning, in my fury at being treated in such a demeaning manner, I walked away. He came after me and tearfully apologized, quoting scriptures, promising it would never happen again. I was an easy mark—besides I knew that leaving him for whatever reason would besmirch my reputation, so it didn't take much to convince me this was a one-time aberration. But in the ensuing years, after the myriad episodes when George repeated this scenario, his promise never to repeat the abuse was hollowed out until finally one day it imploded.

If only I could have had an inkling about God's mercy and grace on all sinners, I might have been saved 17 years of a violent relationship. But George knew that vanity ruled my life and as a proud rule-keeper who didn't believe in divorce, I wouldn't bolt into ostracism. He could treat me pretty much any way he wanted, and then when push came to shove, resort to begging forgiveness, quote 1 John 1:9 ("If we confess our sins, God is faithful and just to forgive us our sins, and to cleanse us from all unrighteousness"), promise to reform and then start all over again. This vicious cycle continued until one day—and by now we had been living in Brazil for 15 years—I asked God, "How much more do you expect me to take?"

The answer, though not audible, was utterly unambiguous, "No more."

Incapable of believing what I had just heard, I rejoined, "You must be kidding. Let's try this one again. I ask the questions. You respond with the platitudes."

But now there was only silence in heaven as I paused and stood on that long porch overlooking a wide, subtropical valley denuded of all the trees that had been there when first we arrived. Still incredulous, I decided to tell God that if what I was hearing was on target then I wanted three rather difficult preconditions met to prove that I was interpreting what I heard correctly.

By the next day all three had happened. My head was whirling, my pride was about to become tattered, but I was in so much emotional pain it somehow didn't matter anymore. I was willing to take on the shame of being a divorcée rather than continue in this tormented relationship. One of the last things George asked me before I left Brazil was how I could justify what I was doing and still call myself a Christian. Looking him straight in the eye I said calmly, "I guess it's because I've prayed for so many years that God would kill you or let you die in an accident or somehow eradicate you from the earth, that I finally decided it was better to do it the way the secular world does it, and merely remove you from my life."

A shocked look settled on his face when it dawned on him how deep-seated was my hatred. Added to this was the fact that by now he had often observed God supernaturally answering my prayers. So he let me go on my way—perhaps strychnine in his soup flitted across his mind. But in all this I learned another important lesson about prayer: you cannot change another person's will.

Choosing to do good or evil are part of the gift of free will given to all humans equally. We must all account one day for our choices—and I have a deep suspicion that it will not go well for cult leaders who try to manipulate and cause the little ones to stumble—but you can't pray another person into good behavior. We all relate directly to our God who has no grandchildren. I also discovered you cannot ask God to punish someone else—no matter what they've done. Judgment is the Lord's bailiwick and comes in God's own timing—unfortunately there seems to be no time limit to God's willingness to be "good even to people who are unthankful and cruel." Scripture even warns us not to gloat when our enemies are being punished, because the Lord will be unhappy with us and stop punishing them (Prov 24:17-18). Of course, even though we have to accept stoically God's being good to our enemies, we can pray for protection, asking the Lord to keep the evildoers away from our door—not forgetting that even Jesus suffered at the hands of the wicked.

The hard part for me was that even though I felt I had been victimized, by walking away I became an outcast in my community—someone rebelling against the male hierarchy that was established by God to keep people like me in my place. It was an easy decision to justify—but virtually no one asked why I was leaving. That I would even contemplate leaving was enough to condemn me. I had a long litany of George's sins, but most of my missionary world didn't want to hear about them. When a few did query, I would start a justifying recital that made such accusers either drop their stones or turn away in shocked silence—some even in tears. I felt vindicated.

Until that perturbing insight flooded over me in the middle of the Jesus Prayer session: I had allowed this pain to enter my life. If I had been willing to say years before, like the publican, "Lord have mercy on me a sinner," I could have walked away free. My 17 years of bondage had not been to an unworthy, abusive, unfaithful spouse; rather they had been to my pride. I had gone on my way thanking God I was not like those cornered, despicable sinners when in reality I was the one caged by my vanity. When I was willing to give up my pride, I was free. My slavery had ended.

The unfortunate corollary to this truth was that I had also judged unmercifully, and now I needed forgiveness. George's sins were not my problems. I didn't keep his ledger or anyone else's. All that was expected of me was to forgive those who despitefully used me—not judge them. If I could have hung in there, letting them beat me about the head and shoulders, I might be a saint by now, but for reasons that I can't understand, God opened the door and let me walk away. God had had more compassion on me than anyone I knew—

but now I had to stop judging and be reconciled to this old adversary.

That morning's Jesus Prayer exercise was so liberating I was floating. During the evening testimony session I got up, propelled out of my seat by the Spirit who moves the recalcitrant, and said, "I'm planning to go to Brazil next month and I need courage to ask an old enemy to forgive me for being judgmental. Please pray that I will be given the supernatural strength I need to pull this one off."

When the service ended friends came up and said, "So you're going to ask George's forgiveness! God bless."

How transparent we are! Within a month I found myself on that same old porch surrounded by tropical flowers and sagging screen doors, facing my old nemesis. With as much grace as I could muster I asked George's forgiveness for having judged him when it really wasn't my place, admitting that I had contributed significantly to the demise of our marriage. I wish I could report that we left friends, but at least we were no longer enemies. I drove back down that washboard dirt road freed from an awesome burden, knowing what I as a Christian was called to do whenever an enemy or adversary crossed my path: merely show mercy.

Mercy is the foundation on which to build a life of prayer. It is vital to grasp the fact that God loves my enemies as much as God loves me because God *is* love. God doesn't love me because I appear to be saintly, or do good works, or go to church a lot. Incredibly— to my way of thinking—God loves me and the most obnoxious, heinous sinner equally. The Lord's forgiveness is available for everyone at the same level. God was being good to me all my life—answering my prayers, filling my life with adventures and good things—not because I was just or obedient or demure. God was doing all this because God is merciful and compassionate and loves me beyond anything I could imagine.

Building on this premise we can go on to comprehend a bit of what patience and longsuffering we are called to by the Gospel. When Peter asked Christ how many times he had to forgive the same person for the same offense, the horrible answer was—not once, not thrice, but "seventy times seven." There is no escaping this prohibition against judging others for their misdeeds. Conversely, recognizing how enslaved we are to our own pride and stubbornness is critical if we are to be merciful to others, for at that point we appreciate how merciful God is to us—every day, every hour.

Which brings us to an important principle of prayer: *God is willing to hear your prayer request because God is merciful, not because you deserve to be heard by being good enough.* In the end we all exist on mercy alone, and the sooner we grasp how much mercy we receive daily from God, the easier it will be to show mercy to all those in our life—not only our family and associates but those we come in contact with peripherally in shops, on the street and in the scurry of our daily life.

PRAYER FOR MERCY

Gracious God, your mercies are new every morning yet so often we ignore them. Thank you for your forbearance and compassion. Help us this day to turn the other cheek when we are confronted by those who would assail us. Let your presence be with us throughout our waking hours so we might go the second mile with those who would be demanding. Give us a supernatural love for our enemies so that we can forgive them their trespasses and so that those who do not know you will see this inconceivable charity and realize such acts must come from you alone. Make us faithful witnesses for your peace, through Christ our Lord. Amen.

2.

A Prayer-Answering God

Praise is due to you, O God, ...
O you who answer prayer! (Ps 65:1)

I'm the kind of person who always wants to know why. If God answers prayer, why? If not, why not? Apparently some type of prayer life is endemic to all cultures, so it would appear that the need to set up a communication system with the Almighty is deeply seated in the human race. Granted there are agnostics and many who have stopped praying in our Western culture, but this is a relatively recent phenomenon for our species. Mostly our ancestors implored the deity as they understood it for health, prosperity, good weather and victory. It either worked or something else convinced them to keep on importuning God down through the ages.

Until I was 13 my prayer life was basically a familial affair. We had family devotions and whenever a crisis appeared, usually my father or mother took the matter to the Lord in prayer. After I was sent off to school, I found myself thrown on my own devices, having to fend for myself in seeking divine intervention. By this time our family had moved to sunny California—a very sinful and worldly place, my parents decided—so a happy solution, for them, was worked out by sending me to that strict Fundamentalist boarding school on the cold, wind-swept plains of Western Canada.

A lot of offspring from missionary families suffered my same fate and were ensconced in this no-frills institution. On being assigned our rooms, we were given a student handbook which contained pages and pages of rules of conduct that had to be observed. Some seemed foolish to me—females couldn't cut their hair because a woman's glory was in her tresses (scripture and verse available for the skeptics); we couldn't wear taps on our shoes (not scripturally based, but still a rule) and girls could only go to town on Tuesdays, Thursdays and Saturdays (so there would be no mingling with the boys, who went on Mondays, Wednesdays and Fridays). No one was allowed in town on Sundays when nothing was open beside the tavern cum billiard hall—which was off limits every day of the week. Boys and girls were not to speak to each other and were strictly separated—we ate in assigned places on two sides of the dining room, sat on opposite sides of the classrooms and chapels and even had separate entrances for all buildings (no accidental collisions).

One of the multitude of regulations heaped on us was a required 30-minute devotional period every morning plus another 15-minutes in the evening—observed by monitors who would creep down the dormitory hallways, flinging open our doors unannounced to make sure we were not ignoring the Scriptures and using the time for homework. In the beginning I tried hard to observe all their rules, but like the damsel in all those fantasy tales I devoured, I fell in with the wrong crowd of girls—all of them American and mostly from wickedly warm California—who started me down the path to perdition. Needing very little encouragement I learned to sneak past the proctors' doors during study hours and share food parcels from home with our friends.

All kinds of tricks of the trade circulated among this racy crowd: If you sat on the top bunk with your Bible open, you could put another book inside a large Bible that would fool any hall monitor who happened to open your door into thinking you were having your devotions when in actuality you were studying or reading a novel—after all, the proctors would scarcely climb up on the bunk to check what page you had your Bible open to. My friends also pointed out that by trimming my bangs bit-by-bit I could continue to wear them and cover my high forehead (it wasn't as though I was pulling any out by the roots causing God to have to do a new hair count).

The absolute worst offense—which I admit took incredible cheek—was to write notes to the boys and pass them back and forth via sister/brother cohorts who were allowed an hour together every Sunday afternoon. I would like to submit that this was before the modern era so none of my wicked crowd of girlfriends was so brazen as to initiate such correspondences—but it did seem rude not to answer when the boys would write us—especially if they were cute!

Every time we were caught in some infraction of an ever-growing list of forbidden behaviors, we were given "detentions" which in the beginning were worked off Saturday mornings by memorizing an allotted portion of Bible verses in an assigned "detention" hall. (I left the school knowing a lot of scripture!) Later the administration changed the rules because they decided we memorized too quickly and it didn't seem as though we suffered sufficiently.

The school was not exceptionally challenging academically and I found I had a lot of time to spare. In the library I could find nary a book I would willingly read except for a stray travelogue or a fictionalized (and scary) account of the coming tribulation and the end of the world. I didn't have pocket money that would allow me to buy much reading material and even though some in our crowd circulated hidden copies of *True Romance*, I felt rather icky reading them.

Suddenly a most serendipitous offer came my way. The manager of the school's bookstore, a longtime family friend, casually mentioned in passing that over the years he had collected a basement full of 30,000 volumes of books and I was welcome to borrow any of them. It was a wonderful boon, for I soon discovered he had every adventure and mystery story known to pique a 13-year-old's imagination. That long winter when the sun would dip below the skyline shortly after we were let out of classes and the cold Arctic winds would whip across the prairies dropping the thermometer as low as 40° below, I could retreat to my upper bunk bed and whiz off to distant (more temperate) lands via these less-than-great books. Every Saturday morning I bundled over to Mr. Durance's house and struggled to choose from his vast corpus of juvenile fiction. I knew my pace, so each week I selected seven titles and the following Saturday would trade them for another seven.

When spring was about to come and the snow began to squish into mud, our war with the administration heated up and turned into a downright antagonistic *Us vs. Them.* Our most heinous deed, which brought about the detention rule change, happened when our gang decided in spite of a late snowstorm to go to town for ice cream cones one afternoon. It was Thursday—our day—besides it's never that cold when it's actually snowing. One of my wicked cohorts suggested we'd better cover up to protect ourselves from the weather. It wasn't the stupidity of this act that caused the consternation, it was that someone in town reported our abhorrent behavior. Since pants were strictly forbidden the female population (Paul's injunction against cross-dressing was the basis for this until it was pointed out that Roman men wore *skirts* in Paul's day!), we had decided to brace ourselves against the snowstorm by wearing our pajama bottoms underneath our overcoats. We had boots on, but if you looked carefully, you could detect a good six inches of pajamas above our boots and below our long coats. It might have worked if Marcia hadn't worn her red-and-white polka-dotted pajamas.

The principal was horrified, the vice-principal was mortified and the proctors were dismayed at our iniquitous behavior. We were marched in one-by-one to the school office for cross-examining. Wire recorders had just come on the market and in an effort to trip us up on our answers, the principal decided to record our sessions so any inconsistencies could be pounced on. Somehow the word got to us, so even though we were kept in the science classroom under the watchful eye of the vice-principal while we awaited our individual turns to be scrutinized (lest we pass on to one another what the third-degree grilling revealed), they never managed to break our system. I still remember the frustrated principal saying, "You mean, yes?" and "You mean, no?" in order to record my bobbing head responses to her queries. My folks would have given me a strict lecture about being so rude to her and not speaking up, but we were too antagonistic at this point to remember our upbringing.

All seven of us received the same punishment, which now was easier than ever. Marcia, whom we had early judged to have the best memory of our lot, must have had a twinge of guilt about the difficulty caused us by her red polka-dotted number so she compensated by demonstrating how she always beat us every Saturday. An eye-saver was the perfect solution—these were fine, coated tissues used for cleaning glasses. Though thin and almost transparent, they were strong enough to write on and then tuck into the sleeve of your sweatshirt without making a bulge. You put the invisible eye-saver over the paper they allowed you to have to write down the prescribed verses while you were memorizing. After surreptitiously transcribing the verses onto the eye-saver, you stashed the tissue and voilà—you cleared your desk of your Bible and all papers and told the proctor you were ready. She'd give you a fresh sheet of school paper on which you were to write the verses and then you could speed through the passage with a peek at your sleeve whenever your memory faltered.

The proctors knew some of us memorized with alacrity, but this was ridiculous—all seven of our gang finished in less than half an hour. No one ever mentioned they suspected us of cheating, but they didn't think we were suffering enough, so after this and forever more it was decided that instead of memorizing the assigned Bible passage, we would have to work off a detention with an hour's added cleaning chore on Saturday mornings. In later years I came to conclude that for me this school proved an excellent Christian reformatory. I went there with no experience of cheating or stealing, but in nine months I had learned to lie, dupe and even shoplift—much to my own dismay.

After that snowstorm fiasco the administration got nastier. The next week when I trundled my books to Mr. Durance's door, instead of inviting me in so I could head down to his basement, he came outside into the frosty morning air and shut the storm door behind him so his wife and boys wouldn't hear our exchange. With tears in his eyes he explained that the principal had called that week to advise him he could no longer lend me books to read. He looked embarrassed when I asked why and then confessed the only reason given him was that since not everyone in the school could read a book a day and keep up on their schoolwork, she had decided it wasn't fair for him to lend books to me just because I could. That was giving me special privileges and there were scriptural injunctions against preferential treatment of the undeserving young.

I never discovered how the principal found out about my book borrowing, but as the Puritans were wont to say, *Idle hands are the devil's handmaidens,* so it was pretty much all-out hostilities from then on. I can only surmise they didn't feel like they were winning many rounds, because the administration seemed to put a lot of energy into being perverse. Soon they appended another addendum to the rule book: we could no longer wear our hair in ponytails. Since we were only allowed to wash our lengthening hair once a week, I had found wearing a ponytail an easy way to keep my not-too-clean hair out of my eyes. Even though I was still prepubescent, the administration decided my ponytail was "provocative" and inappropriate to modest Christian young women so now no one in the school could wear ponytails.

In retrospect, I now realize those people spent an inordinate amount of effort worrying about matters sexual. Today the ubiquitous TV with explicit sexual material shown on daytime programs means our modern youngsters have no comprehension of how uninformed my generation was, but I went to Canada not knowing the facts of life and not really *caring* to know them. Immediately this school began chipping away at my naïveté. During the first week, the school was separated by gender and all were subjected to a hush-hush meeting. I don't know what happened with the boys, but we were basically warned against acting out any homosexual urges. I had read the passage in Romans (1:26-27), but had thought such things had gone out with the Romans. I had no idea such problems still existed—nor did I have any prurient interest in having further details. It did, though, make me gaze around at my consœurs wondering who could possibly practice behavior to warrant this incredible admonition.

We females, in order not to arouse the male side of the school unnecessarily (to do what, they didn't tell, I didn't ask) were told that our dress should in no way aim to make us attractive. Since I had not yet developed it didn't apply to me, but the dean of women explained that one way to keep the male side from lusting after the female side would be to sew in the points of our bras to de-emphasize our female figures (at that juncture I was longing to have one to de-emphasize). Our hair preferably would be captured in a tight bun at the nape of the neck or some suitably prim style and then another couple hundred regulations were added to the pile. The implication was that the females were basically the cause of most sin and if we observed all these rules we would be found pleasing to the Lord. Infractions would lead us to certain doom in this life and failure in the life to come. Other than this they hoped we would be happy at the school and told us to enjoy the rest of the year.

Probably they were trying to break our wills, but their intolerant attitude didn't produce submission; it only made me wonder how they justified their deeds as Christians. The battle raged on, but to the administration's dismay, this in no way made me feel as if I were at war with God. Even though the school officialdom acted as if they were God's mouthpieces, it seemed to me they were just the institute's authorities who had the power to change the rules every time it suited their warped fancy. No "Suffer the little ones to come unto me" stance here, more like the disciples trying to shoo us away. Besides, if they were God's emissaries they would have better answers.

It was their idea for us to do all this scripture reading every morning and evening and with my retentive memory it struck me that we had a problem here. Not only was their behavior hardly exemplary and Christ-like, but the school leaders kept making unjustifiable claims. I read and reread it, took out a pen and wrote the lists down, but it just would not fit. So one day I raised my hand in Bible class and asked why the genealogy of Jesus in Matthew's Gospel didn't match his genealogy in Luke. In chapel lately we had been sitting through some heavy diatribes against all the new translations of the Bible that were then just beginning to appear on the scene—promulgated by modernists who were trying to water down scripture. We had been assured repeatedly that only the King James version brought us the sacred message where every jot and tittle was without error.

I was confused. Since those two genealogies had obviously been jumbled somewhere along the line, how could they claim there were no mistakes in the Bible? There was no way that you could fit those two together. I wanted my whys answered, but instead I was attacked. The Bible teacher, rather than admit she had no reply, acted as though I was trying to set her up out of my unbelief and launched an ad hominem harangue in front of the rest of the ninth graders. My face flushed red. By the time I walked out of class that day I knew that doubts or questions about the Bible were to be kept to myself.

There was even more forbidden territory. On Friday afternoons, to keep the natives from getting restless and to fortify us for the coming weekend, we had a pan-high school testimony meeting. Various ones from the senior class would lead the service and anyone who wanted to praise the Lord could march down front to sit on a side bench and in turn get up and give a public witness to their faith.

In spite of the adversarial role I'd taken vis-à-vis the administration, it didn't occur to me that I was not worthy to praise the Lord. Granted, there had been a few moments of utter despair that year as I got in and out of one scrape after another, but mostly I was a happy camper. Even with the coercion, I did enjoy my devotional times—reading my Bible and praying. Obviously God wasn't as upset with me as the school was, for several times I remember receiving distinct answers to my prayers. Also I had just gotten up during a service led by Major Ian Thomas from Capenwray, England, when he asked all those willing to allow the Holy Spirit to take charge of their lives from that day forward to make a public stand. Major Thomas had explained to us that it was important to declare our faith, so one sunny spring Friday I screwed up my courage and trooped down to sit on the bench during the testimony meeting. When my turn came I stood up and praised God for some answer to prayer—now forgotten—because I felt so grateful to know that the God of the universe was willing to be in communication with me.

Though I can't remember the incident that prompted my being willing to make a public spectacle of myself in order to thank the Lord in front of my classmates, what resulted is imprinted for life. School dismissed daily with announcements that came over the building's loudspeaker system. The following Monday afternoon the entire school heard the stern voice of our infamous principal reciting the day's news. She finished in icy tones requesting that I appear in her office immediately. Usually I knew what I had been caught doing, but this time I was genuinely baffled. My friends shot me looks that silently asked, "What now?"

The blank-faced school secretary nodded me into the inner sanctum where I sat in my customary chair. I was dumbfounded to hear the caustic tones in the principal's voice as she berated me for having the nerve to testify in public. She reproached me, a byword of the boy's dormitory, for thinking that God would possibly answer my prayers.

When I walked out of her office I was determined to do two things: look up the definition of "byword" and never discuss my faith again anywhere where people like her could judge me. The bifurcation was complete: how the school administrators viewed the expression of their faith and how I perceived mine had very little in common. I knew I was in no position to call them to repentance—besides, they had all the power on their side—but I also knew that God answered my prayers and that my communication system with the Lord was not dependent on whether or not the principal was happy with me.

I was willing to admit I wasn't perfect, but it obviously wasn't a prerequisite. Who were they to talk? They got angry all the time, spent enormous amounts of energy judging everything that moved and certainly didn't do much forgiving even one time, let alone seventy times seven. Who gave them permission to be so suspicious and mean? Not a few verses in the Gospels I had read in all our devotional time were obviously being ignored here! What about: "Be ye kind one to another"? Being school officials didn't exempt them from the Gospels, so if they didn't want to accept the validity of God's interactions in my life, obviously I didn't need to give much credence to them when they pontificated on what it meant to live your faith. They had issued the general call asking any who wanted to testify to what God was doing in our lives to let others know how thankful they were. They plainly weren't being forthright if this excluded my ilk.

At the end of the school year I picked up my report card with straight As in everything except deportment—which I had failed for the year. The school also apprised my parents that I was not welcome to return the next year—which I saw as a relief ("all things work together for good...") but which my mother took as a slur on her name. I proceeded to warmer climes for the rest of my high school education, trying to put behind me that harsh year in that Spartan setting with the almost-cultic efforts made to demean and humiliate those who refused to be quiescent lambs.

Even though I wasn't inclined to talk about it much after that, I left Canada convinced God continued to answer my prayers—regardless of my deportment grades. I didn't know why, but I could tell the Lord was paying attention when I prayed. Years later it became clearer to me: God loves to do good things for us when we ask because God loves to answer our prayers. It's as simple as that. I had been raised in a society where it seemed everyone loved to say no and confront the world wearing hair shirts, but my experience of God was at variance with this stance.

By the time I figured all this out, I was living at the end of the jungle trail on Brazil's frontier where it took twelve hours from the nearest asphalt, bouncing along gutted dirt roads, to get to my sprawling home under its canopy of flowering trees and my passel of kids. Times were I wondered what I'd ever done to deserve the affliction of living in such a remote corner of God's green earth. True, my days were so filled with caring for ten children, trying to run a home with no electricity, water that had to be pulled out of a well and a life at the margins of modernity, there was little time for cogitating on anything other than obligations. But I was still trying to keep up with my morning devotions and evening prayer life, which allowed me a certain space for reflection on my life.

Mostly my days were chockablock full. I baked bread in an outdoor beehive-shaped brick oven. (You heated it by burning lots of firewood inside this home-made brick grotto. When the raised bread was ready to be baked, you scraped out all the burning coals replacing them with the raised loaves and then sealed in the heat with a small door wedged against the bricks with a stick.) I churned cream to make butter. (I learned lessons no one ever taught me in college — like cream must be 24-hours old and cooled to 50° before it will turn into butter!) I made cheese. (You mustn't scrimp on rinsing the curds with a lot of water after they have congealed and separated from the whey unless you want your cheese to taste sour.) Cooking endless meals, cleaning and washing, plus keeping track and meeting the needs (as best I could) of ten active children, left me little time to myself for years. (I'm the only one in my crowd who, while reading Laura Ingalls Wilder to the kids at bedtime, used to check out the stories for recipes and ideas to help survive in my tropical wilderness.)

29

But during the hot, steamy summer afternoons my Nordic genes took over and my will collapsed. Then I would retreat to our porch overlooking the wide, sultry valley that fell away from our house on the crest of the hill and sit, yearning for the slightest whiff of moving air to cool my brow. Since being idle is foreign to my nature, I would hunker down in the hammock to meditate, read or sew. One day I took a notebook to the porch and on an impulse began to jot down ideas. Suddenly I decided I was going to try my hand at writing and soon came that wonderful mail day—we only got mail once or twice a month—when I was handed a slim envelope. It was never to be surpassed by any subsequent writing triumph. I had sent off my first article and here it was: an acceptance letter—on my first try.

A piece entitled "Had Your Miracle Today?" came out in a rather conservative journal. The charismatic wars were tearing asunder the evangelical world, so I was surprised the editor chose that transcendent line out of my piece to substitute for my own restrained title. My thesis was that one of the surest ways to guarantee your children would know that God is alive and well is to let them see how God answers prayers—concretely and in their own lives.

Since I was in the midst of my child-rearing years, I was concerned about how you pass on your faith. My article posited that the prayer requests didn't have to be huge, just perceivable by your family members. As in my measles episode, I knew that if my children could experience God as willing to interact daily in their lives, answering mundane (but looming large on their horizon) prayers, it would be impossible for them to deny an existential God. The publisher of this magazine also had ten children. I was a lot younger, of course, but still we were both faced with having to impart our faith to ten very different individuals—some who early had their hearts turned toward the Lord and others who remained aloof.

What exactly makes one keep the faith? I mused on this subject over the years as I watched various friends from my Christian boarding school days turn their backs completely on the church that had tried to nurture us in the admonition of the Lord. Why had I, who could have easily won a "Least Likely to Be a Missionary" award at every school I attended, given up the bright lights to raise all these children in the hinterland of Brazil while my more virtuous colleagues had walked away from any outward expression of their faith? Longevity not having been my best suit at the Christian boarding schools I attended, I had managed to interface with a lot of young people sent off to be bolstered in the fear of the Lord. With my lifelong "attitude problem," I was inclined to hang out with a mutinous crowd, but why had I parted company with so many of my classmates who now never darkened the door of a church?

Thinking back, I realized I'd taken my ire out on the schools. God had been left out of the fight, so there was no need to repudiate my faith in God—just in those institutions. I also concluded that though I had aggravated many with my constant questioning of temporal authority—before anyone had coined the term or printed the bumper sticker—still I had always known God was not as displeased with me as they were. Somehow I could intuit that their rules were a lot more important to them than they were to God. Besides, issues that the Bible concentrated on, and that seemed essential to the Lord, were ones these school administrators tended to slough off—like humility and loving your neighbor and not offending the little ones. With all my flagrant infractions of the school's petty rules, I had never questioned God's existence or involvement in my life—except for one black day during my senior year in high school when I had to spend Christmas vacation at my school in Florida because it was too "expensive" to bring me home to California. The days were rather cold and empty. I remember the angst that swept over me as I wondered if it wasn't sheer arrogance to posit that God existed. How could we possibly know?

By the next day I had answered my own question: Of course there was a God. After all, who else was answering all my prayers down through the years with such frequency and specificty that you knew it could not possibly be coincidental?

It also seemed obvious that since those school administrators ped-dled themselves as paragons of Christian virtue, it was understandable why my schoolmates faded away from the organized church where these types were prone to dominate. I was delivered from this total revolt because my early prayer life had proved to me the validity of Scripture—regardless of how Christian leaders chose to act. Time and again I had asked God to intervene on my behalf in problems large and small. Consistently God would answer these requests. Through the years as I observed miraculous assistance and provisions take place, my faith had been strengthened.

How could I ignore this God who was so mixed up in my life? How could I not reciprocate and get mixed up in serving this wondrous Lord who didn't seem to mind that I wasn't especially pliant or tractable? I was captivated by this God who answered my prayers because of an immense and undeserved love for me. After all, while we were yet sin-ners Christ died for us. He didn't heal the people that were good, he healed those who were sick and said "please." He liked them to say "thank you" ("Where are the other nine?"), but he didn't take away their healing when they didn't mind their manners.

Basically I knew the experience of God answering their prayers would hook my children for life on a personal relationship to the Lord. I regretted that my upstanding institutional friends had lost much of the vision of what God was all about. They could keep—and impose—rules, but in the process they had forgotten the essentials: "By this shall everyone know that you are my disciples, that you love one another." My God was not a rule keeper; otherwise why was the Syrian leper healed and the Syro-Phoenician widow fed? Why did the disciples walk about *and* eat on their Sabbath? And Christ socialize with sinners? Why did the publican, the one with the most detentions, the "byword" in the village, go home forgiven while the distinguished rule keeper, the eminent the-ologian, the church elder left still burdened down with a load of pride?

In Brazil as I mused on my life during those torpid summer after-noons, I realized it was another miracle that as the girl who had racked up the most detentions for the year, I had not tossed it all over like many others of my set who decided that if this is Christianity, they didn't need it. The bedrock conviction that God was going to be there for me today and tomorrow as surely as the Lord had been there for me yesterday, miraculously intervening on my behalf over and over again, kept me going during the many rough spots. Raising these children with a dearth of the creature comforts I had known gave me abundant opportunities to turn to God in prayer. I needed divine intervention as I went about my tasks—cooking, cleaning, washing and eternally improvising so that we might survive under the stresses that come from living in the jungles where three-day tropical rainstorms were common. When supplies ran low and everything stayed damp or mildewed so I had to iron diapers dry with a charcoal-filled iron, then I saw God graciously intervene.

My God was beyond finding out and much more merciful and gracious and willing to help in time of trouble than any human being I had encountered. For this reason I felt that whatever it seemed God was asking of me I should do. If it meant saying yes when asked to adopt eight children who were falling through the cracks, so be it. If it meant living hours away from the nearest corner of civilization—I guess that was fine, too. Not always without grumbling, but I could do all those things because I remembered not only the measles incident, but all the other times down through the years when I would stop and say, "Let's pray and ask God to help." The answers were spectacularly affirmative enough times to make me confident that God was alive and interested in keeping my life afloat by providing physically—food, raiment and a lot more besides.

I found I could ask God to help me with my most mundane problems. When I first got the kids, there was a tall stately woman—obviously with some Watusi ancestors—who came to the house each week and carted our laundry to a nearby creek. There she pounded our dirty clothes clean at water's edge, then laid them out on the rocks or nearby bushes to dry. A day or two later she would come down the trail balancing a huge bundle of clean clothes on top of her head. Since she used a coal-burning iron, our laundry always had a smokey tinge to it. The bad part was that all the clothes were wearing out what with the normal wear-and-tear from healthy, active kids compounded by the rigors of the washing at the stream. Finally it dawned on me that I should stop complaining and asked God to please give me a washing machine. Part of me wasn't even surprised when within days some departing Americans bequeathed on us their ingenious old-fashioned wringer washing machine that had been rigged up to a pulley that ran off a small gasoline lawn mower engine.

It was a bit noisy, but wash days became almost like a party. We had to wait for good weather, but I organized and put our 16 or 17 loads of weekly wash through the machine and the two rinses in the concrete washtub while the kids scurried around doing the various chores: carting water, grating the home-made lye soap so it would dissolve in water, making the open-air fire to heat the water in 20-liter kerosene cans, and then hanging the clothes out in that blazing tropical sun. Usually by the time we had gotten to the 16th load, the first loads were already flapping dry and ready to be brought in and folded. I never made the lye soap myself but whenever we needed soap we would butcher a pig and I would barter the prized fat with someone who agreed to return an appropriate amount of lye soap.

Thus because of that simple prayer, I was convinced God had provided a means to solve what I perceived to be an irritating laundry problem. Such answers to my prayers egged me on to ask God for more and more concrete solutions to the many difficulties inherent in raising such a large family in the jungles.

Some of my friends thought it was stupid for me to think the God who created this vast universe would be interested in the slightest whether I had meals on the table or money to pay my washerwoman. Their God had wound up the cosmos and gone away to brood over other waters. It was sheer arrogance, they felt, for me to bring to God my trifling difficulties. But I knew the God who watched every spar-

row fall from the sky, who knew my physical state a lot more intimate-
ly than I did—for not even after calculus did I have a clue as to how
many hairs I had on my head—this God who made all the rules that
kept the stars orbiting and the ants working and the flowers blooming
did care whether my children ate three meals a day, whether there was
water in the tank so I could wash their clothes and whether or not the
pickup could make it to town one more time so I could stock up on
groceries (and get my mail).

It seemed obvious to me that this was Biblical. "O, ye of little faith."
All through the years of my growing up, time and again the Lord had
answered specific prayers in specific ways. Because my parents were
missionaries and there never was much money around, many of my
early prayer requests dealt with financial matters—like my junior year
in college when I was in the women's glee club. During spring break we
were to go on a concert tour to Miami and back. Churches where we
would sing were arranged at convenient intervals along the way and
they in turn would house us, giving us supper and breakfast every day.
Lunches were to be our own responsibility. I prayed and asked the
Lord for my expense money but I also wrote my parents telling them
of my need. Mother sent back a letter with a check for $8.28. She was
sorry it couldn't be more, but she had spoken at a ladies' aid meeting
and they had taken up an offering and given her this check which she
endorsed to me.

It wasn't a lot, but this was 1960 and in those days you could get
paper-thin hamburgers for 19 cents at the new fast-food outlets which
were quickly becoming ubiquitous. I decided this would see me
through if I was totally frugal. Then just as the bus was pulling away
from campus amidst much jovial leave-taking (we'd all just finished
our exams), a girlfriend in my dorm handed me an envelope and told
me not to read the letter until we were underway. I was shocked. This
was the only time in my college career it happened thus, but I opened
the letter to find $50 inside. In the accompanying note my classmate
said she felt the Lord wanted her to give me this gift for my trip. I was

ecstatic to think that God would not only answer my prayers, but meet my needs so generously.

Somewhere in our southern exposure I ate something at a church supper that gave me food poisoning. That night in Athens, Georgia, my roommate and I were housed with a couple from the church where the host happened to be a doctor, his wife a nurse. We were shown to one corner of their large, sprawling house where we had our own bath. Even though I tried to be quiet about it, I was up all night being sick. Our hostess must have heard me because the next morning when I dragged myself out of bed, she told me she had just called our choir director to tell her I was too sick to get on that bus. She thought if I laid low for awhile, I would probably be well enough to rejoin the choir the following day. I'd miss one concert but could meet up with them in Miami. Mrs. Mac, our choir director, said if it were anyone else, she'd say no, but since I had traveled so much and was so independent, she agreed that under the circumstances it was the best game plan.

I went back to bed and by afternoon had slept off most of what had ailed me. My hostess greeted me with an iced drink and the news that the next morning she was driving across the border to her son's school in Jacksonville, Florida, to pick him up for Easter break. She had gotten the bus schedule for Jacksonville and we could go early enough to make connections so I could get a bus from there to Miami in time for our concert. It worked out perfectly. When I stepped up to the ticket counter and asked for a one-way fare to Miami, the agent said, "That will be $8.28."

This stunning news floated me all the way to Miami. Here the Lord, who knew everything, cared enough not only to provide my needs generously, but had let my mother give me just the right amount for this extra bus fare that I had not anticipated. During the concert that evening, as always, there was a chance for a few spontaneous testimonies. I usually ducked that one, but I was so excited about this penny-perfect provision, I told the story about asking the Lord for my expense money on this trip and my mother's check for exactly the amount needed for this unexpected bus ticket.

After the concert when we were disrobing, a senior in the choir who was also an officer of the group came up to tell me how embarrassed she was by what I had said. She thought it had been tacky for me to talk about money. I gave her a sullen answer and turned away thinking how really unhappy she would be if she knew that as I left the sanctuary that evening a little old lady had come up to thank me for my testimony and then shook my hand, pressing a ten-dollar bill into it. Once again I got the picture—if you are in communication with God, most people in the church prefer not to hear about it. I shrugged off her complaints and from then on tried to keep my mouth shut.

In all this I discovered there is no way you can program God's answers to your prayer. Another time during my senior year in college I totally ran out of money. I wasn't in the dorms so didn't have a meal ticket which meant I paid cash for the food I ate. When I realized I was running low, I'd written my parents, but they hadn't responded. I was working at the college 20 hours a week, but for some reason my paycheck was late. No baby-sitting jobs had recently shown up, but I kept hoping something would turn up. After two days of subsisting on crackers and tea which I brewed in my room, I finally got disgusted and went to the financial aid office where they said, "Of course, no problem," handing me a $50 emergency loan. Thinking about this incident, I decided the Lord was trying to tell me not to expect every answer to prayer to fall out of the sky. I had to exhaust all the possibilities there were, swallow my pride when necessary and ask for a loan. Just because rather spectacular provisions had come my way sometimes did not exempt me from my responsibilities.

Then the month after I graduated from college I married George, an engineer from Texas working in the aerospace industry in Southern California. At the time my parents were missionaries in Brazil but they came for the wedding—which my dad performed. After they went back to Brazil we moved into a home in North Hollywood which my parents had owned for several years. Within a year we had joined my parents in Brazil as self-supporting missionaries—meaning that we would be serving the mission my father had founded, but would have to pay our own travel expenses and live on a monthly allowance of $50.

This went a lot further in 1962 than it does today, but I had basic doubts about this upcoming adventure. To slow it down a bit I asked the Lord to give us $2,000 beyond our plane tickets as a sign we were supposed to go. The very next day George came home from work to announce that because the race for the moon was on, he was being asked to work 72 hours a week—which about doubled his salary. Within a couple months we had amassed the extra $2,000 and I felt I had nowhere to hide. I responded to this rather miraculous provision just as doubtfully as Gideon had and told the Lord that $2,000 didn't seem like much. What about another thousand—please?

We were getting organized to leave the country and I was finishing my practice teaching to get my secondary credential before our departure. A few days later as I drove down a dirt road behind the university on a shortcut to get to the high school where I taught one class a day, an old duffer in a pickup, who had his eye on the baseball practice going on in the field behind me, suddenly swung wide onto the road and sideswiped the entire length of my car. It wasn't worth that much and we had thought it might be hard to sell when we left, but we had the damage assessed and the insurance settled for $650—which was top dollar for the car. We pasted it together with baling wire and drove it until we left, at which time we junked the car because with the damaged body no one wanted it.

Just prior to leaving for Brazil we went to Texas to spend a week with my in-laws. While there, a neighbor who had the key to our house in California called to give us the bad news that the hose on our washing machine had burst, spewing hot water all over our bungalow. Firefighters had come and turned off the hot water and she was trying to air it out, but there appeared to be water damage on all the floors. Back home I called our insurance agent. He said he was sorry, our policy did not cover water damage. He was a good Christian buddy of my dad's, but just in case, I took out the policy, read the fine print and called him back. He claimed he was just about to telephone me because he was double-checking our policy, and sure enough hot-water damage *was* covered. After the adjustor examined the harm done, they sent us a check for $350. I cleaned and waxed the stained linoleum, shampooed the rug and decided the new renters could probably live with it. That made the extra $1,000 I'd prayed for, but from then on whenever I was asking God for money, I tried to remember to put in a clause requesting it not come from insurance damage — just too traumatic a way to have your needs met.

During those frenzied days, it wasn't just money I prayed for. Even though my father and George were thoroughly enthusiastic about what a wonderful contribution we could make to the Brazil enterprise, the whole adventure made no sense to me. When the Brazilian consulate began to give us run-arounds as we tried to apply for permanent visas, I prayed, asking the Lord that if we were to go to Brazil to serve with my folks' mission, please to work it out so that our permanent visas would be granted before we left. The hassles the consulate gave us were just a foretaste of all the red tape to come, but it did seem a total miracle when the morning of the day our flight was scheduled to leave, we were called to come pick up our permanent visas.

Of course the graduate program in prayer started nine months after getting to Brazil when we adopted the eight children — eight concrete incentives to establish a fervent prayer life. In subsequent years, every time I felt discouraged about our life in Brazil, I had all those initial miracles to cling to. For some reason the Lord had opened the doors miraculously, so obviously I was meant to be in Brazil doing what I was doing. I could only conclude that if the God of the universe was willing to provide and intercede in my life as Jesus had taught, I was willing to follow.

On those hot afternoons on my porch as I thought about the daily miracles in our lives and wrote that first article, I knew this was the means by which I would pass on my beliefs. If I wanted my children to grow in faith and trust, they needed to see God act daily in their own lives. I encouraged them to ask for God's intervention in their own day-to-day needs. Seeing miracles happen thus became as customary for them as they were for me. When they would come and tell me about a worry, a dream or ask for something that I couldn't give them, I'd respond, "Have you prayed about it?" If they wanted, I'd stop right then and pray with them about whatever was troubling them—usually reminding them that God was willing to deal with them directly, so they needed to establish their own communication lines with the Lord.

I have come to believe that God bothers with our inconsequential problems because not only does the Lord love to answer our prayers, but also because God wants to get our attention. God is interested in setting up a communication system with all of us—a relationship, not of peers, but one where we come asking. After all Scripture says, "If you, being evil, won't give your child a stone when asked for bread, how much more, you of little faith, . . ." (Mt 7:9). For years I have assured my children, and now my grandchildren, based on valid experience that the God who loves me beyond my power to imagine, who walked in the cool of the evening with our progenitors, who is totally other and beyond anything we could imagine, wants to be in relationship with them as well.

Which brings us to another principle of prayer: *God answers our prayers because the Lord wants to set up an intimate, loving relationship with each of God's creatures.*

There are a few cautions that can be added. I have learned and have stressed to my children that we must never be tempted to think that just because we are in communication with God through prayer, we will no longer have any more difficulties. Since God is love and it would be lovely not to have any problems, we must not assume that this loving God will rid our lives of any troubles. Such expectations lead to popular books being written about why bad things happen to good people.

A Christian can hardly rest comfortably in such platitudes because the most cursory examination of our faith would indicate that our loving God sent an extraordinarily loved part of the Godhead in the person of Jesus Christ to live here on earth and then die a most cruel death for the singular crime of being a do-gooder. "Better that one die than all of us suffer," said the authorities to justify their spiteful behavior. When there were no legions of angels sent to intervene in this suffering, "He helped others, but he can't help himself!" was the conclusion.

Recently I published the collected writings of a remarkably gifted young woman who died at 18 of cancer (Patty Smith, *Mango Days: A Teenager Facing Eternity Reflects on the Beauty of Life*). Her musings collected from her journals and letters about what was happening to her, about her faith and her approaching death have proven to be a powerful tool of ministry to those who read it. We even received a letter from some-one who was handed this book on the eve of a planned suicide but who abandoned her scheme because reading Patty's journal somehow made life more precious.

The author's mother is a woman of prayer who has been a source of inspiration to me. I'll never forget a talk we had once about the problem of pain and going through real Golgotha experiences. She described an imagery that came to her once when she was tempted to ask, Why? It seems, she feels, as though every time we ask God an accusatory Why? we shrivel, becoming smaller and denser. But every time we praise God (which is the flip side of trusting God) we expand, becoming lighter and "lacier."

This lovely metaphor has been a powerful stimulus when daily I am tempted not to trust God. Of course! God wants us to mount up with wings as eagles, to become lighter and to trust instead of worry. To say "please" and "thank you" instead of becoming heavier, constricted people who refuse to place our confidence in the God who has made us so wondrously and put us in such a lovely world. In becoming "lacier" we not only set up a communication process with the Creator of the Universe, we also develop a listening ear so we can start to obey the still, small voice that comes to prod us on our journey of faith—so that at the end of the trail we might hear the welcome, "Enter!"

PRAYER OF PRAISE

Loving God, you surround us daily with signs of your presence. We bring you our problems, our needs, our sorrows and our petitions. Because we have so often received succor from you in time of distress, we, your unworthy servants, come boldly asking that we might again receive, expecting anew to see the evidence of your loving attention to us. We praise you and bless you for all the times that we perceive your bountiful intervention in our lives. Give us truly thankful hearts and grant that we may learn to trust you a bit more each day. Make us worthy to be called your servants, through Christ our Lord. Amen.

3.

God's Provision

"One does not live by bread alone."

(Mt 4:4)

This is what Jesus replied at the end of his 40-day wilderness fast when the devil taunted him, "If you are the Son of God, command this stone to become a loaf of bread."

When you are hungry and in want, the temptation is to start blaming God for your circumstances. Remembering that we do not live by bread alone was not an easy lesson for me to learn. It didn't take long to realize, as I was trying to raise all those children, that I spent most of my energy in the area of Christ's first temptation—getting bread. Feeding eight hungry and active children on a budget of $50 a month meant that I constantly had to ask God for provision.

I backed into parenting those children having never seriously contemplated raising any children. I married right out of school and felt too young to have a family, so decided to go on with my studies. Then our plans blew up. Years later they admitted there had been collusion, but at the time I was snookered. My father, the president of a small Lutheran mission in Brazil, was visiting in the States and staying with us for a few days. He started putting pressure on me to come to Brazil

43

to help out with the mission project, claiming the American children down there were in dire need of a good teacher. Whenever I mentioned that I was training to be a high school teacher and these kids were mostly in grade school, he answered that since I could do about anything I put my mind to, I shouldn't worry. I proceeded to ask what possible task a space engineer like George could fulfill in the Brazilian jungles, but my dad sloughed off the question and said plenty of work existed for everyone.

There was a certain appeal to the idea of living within the protective reach of my family. Because of George's abusive behavior—which I was too embarrassed to talk about with anyone—I was feeling bereft. I hoped being closer to my parents would give George incentive to curb his temper, but of course it didn't. Worse, not only did the abuse continue, but a few years after we got to Brazil I found I had to deal with the added agony of his being unfaithful with a young Brazilian girl. My Christian upbringing had not prepared me for this. I had no escape hatch, no back door, no one even to discuss all this with. He was a missionary, after all. Serving the Lord. A few aberrant scenes, true, but George felt that when he said he was sorry, my Christian obligation was to forgive and forget. Besides, he assured me he would never, ever. . . .

Still, I couldn't understand where George's enthusiasm for moving to South America came from. It took 15 years—just as I was planning to leave Brazil—for the truth to fall out. Apparently, as the "little woman" I was undeserving of the truth back then. The real motivation for our going to Brazil was that my dad had offered to make his new son-in-law the manager of two rather large mission farms which had been purchased by various members of our family plus friends who, like the early Congregational missionaries in Hawaii, were hoping to do good (supporting worthy mission projects) while doing well (getting in on the coffee market when it was still being called *ouro verde*—"green gold").

Had I known, I would have pointed out the folly of this double-minded choice, but I wasn't consulted. Not comprehending how thousands of acres of land could bewitch *any*one, I had no reason to suspect where the staggering enthusiasm was coming from as the two men in my life—both of whom expected me to be subservient—kept assuaging my every doubt. Finally with all the pressure, I naïvely agreed to go along with their plan. What was keeping me in the States? I'd finished college, had no meaningful job and my parents were already in Brazil. So, barely six months after my father's visit and a year after marrying George, I found myself at the airport, sobbing almost uncontrollably—some part of my soul must have intuited what lay ahead—as my friends and relatives tried to assure me it would be okay.

But it wasn't! Soon we were deep in the jungles of Brazil, living with my parents—there was no separate housing available when we arrived. We were stuck with this infelicitous choice since now I had my resentful mother to deal with on a daily basis. Being a missionary was the only career choice I knew about, and at the back of my mind I always assumed that some day I'd be one, but when I was in college I did all the research papers I could on Pakistan because when you look at a map, that is about as far as you can get from Brazil without going extraterrestrial. It didn't take a genius to figure out that my mother held an intense, inexplicable animosity towards me, so if I wanted a tranquil life, best locate myself at far remove from Brazil. (She was later diagnosed as being paranoid, but at the time I just knew she worked overtime making my life miserable.)

Shortly after our arrival, my mother made it clear how furious she was that my father had "allowed" me to come to Brazil to "ruin" everything. There were already nine American families living on this 6,000 acre plot of jungle—not doing much "good" by anyone's standards and most of them at loggerheads with at least one or more of the others. To keep up even a modicum of an American life-style in this world of no electricity and haphazard services meant that an inordinate amount of time was spent simply surviving—hauling water, fixing motors, baking bread, feeding chickens, butchering, hunting, driving almost impassable roads for 35 miles (three to four hours on good days) to the closest market town for supplies. Besides this, someone had to supervise the Brazilian farm workers who were involved in planting thousands of coffee trees as the rain forest was cleared, acre by burning acre.

It wasn't culture shock that got me, it was mission shock. The rumored educational needs of the community had been grossly exaggerated. The two high-school-aged boys were utterly uninterested in studying under any tutelage. They spent all their waking hours in the jungles "hunting." Their parents felt they were progressing as well as could be expected on their correspondence courses and could see no reason to impose classroom discipline on them at this stage. The grade-school-aged children all happened to have at least one parent who was an *experienced* teacher and none of them felt the need to switch from their parent-administered correspondence courses to a neo-phyte like me. One four-year-old who didn't know how to read was sent down the path to me a couple mornings a week to learn his ABCs, but that was it.

This gave me plenty of time to wonder how these squabbling, mean-spirited people could justify coming a quarter of the way around the world to act in such an unChristlike manner. The logical thing for me to do at this juncture would have been to lobby for a return to America, but I couldn't forget the phenomenal answers to prayer which we had received on the eve of our leaving the States—the extra money and our permanent visas. These miraculous answers to prayer—albeit unusual—led me to feel that for reasons I couldn't understand, God had brought us to Brazil.

After we had been in the tropics some five months, old family friends from Minnesota ventured a visit. My folks decided they needed to see the famous Iguaçu Falls, a hundred miles away as a crow flies, but a trip that took about 16 hours zigging and zagging around road-less jungles. Since we hadn't been to these spectacular falls yet, George and I were invited to come along. It would be a long day's journey, we were warned, but it turned out a bit more harrowing than anticipated. Everyone got up early to scramble on the back of our jeep pickup which was supposed to take us to the nearest grassy airstrip. When we got to the local Xambrê River we found half the bridge had just sunk a foot below the water level. A canted bus was still on the bridge, its rear tires half in, half out of the water.

A riverside observer reported that the day before someone had dived off this bridge, which was barely above water level, and hit his head or somehow drowned in the murky water. The superstitions in the interior around dead bodies were never-ending, so no one was willing to go in and fetch the body which had lodged firmly underneath the bridge. Some tried to fish the corpse out with poles, but it was stuck. Finally the bright idea was proposed to cut a manhole in the bridge and yank the body out from above. In doing this, the primitive bridge structure was so weakened that when a loaded bus crossed that morning, the weight sank the pilings, almost tumbling the bus into the river. Everyone had scrambled to safety but a glance convinced you no one would be moving soon across that bridge.

Boards had been put down to make a foot bridge, so the six of us grabbed our suitcases and walked the teetering plank to hitchhike the next leg of the journey on the bed of an empty rice truck which had to turn around without a load at the bridge—it would come back in a day or two when the repairs were completed. We were rushing to make a noon plane that finally showed up at three—which in turn ferried us over part of the jungle to a bus line that would take us to the falls.

At that time all the roads in the state were like spokes in a wheel leading to Curitiba, the capital, so it was very difficult to get from one spoke to the next. I managed to get us loaded on the wrong, overly crowded bus where we were standing squished in the aisles. My Portuguese wasn't good enough to realize that *"de Iguaçu"* meant "from Iguaçu", but fortunately the sun was already low enough in the sky so my dad announced over the heads of the 20 or so hot and grubby locals who crowded between us that we were headed east when we should be going west. The bus driver stopped on the outskirts of this little town in front of a sawmill and the owner graciously ferried six weary Americans back to town so we could get on the proper bus.

That bus only broke down once in the middle of a tropical downpour which turned the dirt road into a slithering mud bath. Finally we were delivered at midnight to the grand old hotel at the falls some 22 kilometers outside the town by a taxi driver who tried desperately to cheat us. The hotelier claimed not to have any more rooms, but we said that *something* had to be available, we were not moving. They finally offered us a dormitory-style suite normally reserved for students. It had two bedrooms, each with four bunk beds plus a bathroom shared in-between. We said fine. So for the grand sum of five dollars each we had three sumptuous meals in beautiful surroundings—and these Spartan digs.

It was splendid. We had electricity, hot running water, a swimming pool, waiters in white linen jackets serving us breakfast on a tropical patio overlooking the falls replete with a pet monkey who eyed our plates to see if there was anything he would deign to beg or steal. The others went touristing to Paraguay and Argentina (just across the river), but all George and I did was swim, laze around the pool and read. After three days of reflecting and pondering the awful situation back at the *fazenda* (which after all had been named after me *Fazenda Santa Fé*—in Portuguese since the English doesn't quite fly—Holy Faith Ranch), I told George that something had to happen. Then I suggested we simply pray and ask God to take off the farm all those Americans who weren't dedicated to serving the Lord and the work of our mission. It was ridiculous to think that anything positive for God's kingdom could happen under the current circumstances.

That simple prayer marked the beginning of the most extraordinary exodus. Within two weeks the first American left—an emergency trip because of a stepfather's death and the need to support an aging mother. The next three months saw everyone except for one family—and my folks—leave. Although I was impressed by how powerful prayer could be, I still hadn't figured out how precise you had to be when you prayed.

I had forgotten the orphanage.

One of my father's irks—which I heard about plenty while eating at his dinner table—centered on an older couple who had decided while he was away in the States to start an orphanage. Even 30 years ago everywhere you looked there were Brazilian children abandoned, neglected or at risk. Papa, as mission president, didn't think they should have assumed the authority to begin such an energetic project without his approval. But they had sailed along, ignoring protocol, saying they would raise the necessary funds and rather quickly they found a backer who paid for lumber and tile.

Soon an eager crew had erected a primitive but large building to house 24 very small orphans (no one thought about how fast children grow, but long-term planning was not the forté of anyone involved in this project). This home had just been finished when I arrived in Brazil and the couple had begun the "orphanage" work with three children—two sisters, four and eight, plus a brother, seven. Their father had been killed in a barroom brawl by their mother's boyfriend. He got off on self-defense but wanted nothing to do with his rival's children, so their mother rummaged around looking for somewhere to leave them. When she heard about the American orphanage abuilding she gathered up the three and dropped them off, cum birth certificates (the only requirement aside from relinquishing any rights to the children henceforth) and headed back down the trail to live with her boyfriend.

Not long after we got back from our adventure to the falls, this older couple announced they were too infirm to carry on orphanage work in Brazil and needed to return to the U.S. for their health's sake. Not six months had elapsed since they had begun this venture, but she was a real troublemaker so no one was exactly sorrowful when the tidings went out. Rumor had it that once while my parents were traveling she and another American missionary woman—now departed from the scene—had such an altercation that one of them had torn the other's blouse off. In fact, it was hearing this story that had prompted my prayer request at the falls.

But at this news my antennae went up. Who would care for the three children? I started pestering my father about what was being planned for the orphans. To my astonishment, within days of our arrival in Brazil my father had invited George to sit on the local Mission Committee that met weekly to chart the course and decide who was going to do what. This seemed a presumptuous move to me, smacking of nepotism, but no one seemed to question Papa's decision. I wasn't allowed at these meetings, but I had other access. Soon every meal—a great time for captive audiences—was salted with my dire warnings about what God would do to those who abandon orphans, who starting to plow, look back, etc. (all those detention Scriptures were rolling back on their heads).

The orphanage directors kept assuring one and all that "God would provide" someone to take over the work. In fact they were so confident of this that *after* they had decided to return to the States, they proceeded to accept five more children into the orphanage. I was aghast. How could the Mission Committee let them get away with such irresponsible behavior? My father, who has been called one of the gentlest people to walk on the face of the earth (though I assure you, my mother was not among this crowd), was constitutionally incapable of stopping this imbroglio from occurring. Since the jungle drums were still beating out the news that the Americans were taking in children, almost daily little jeeps, horse-drawn carts or even bicycles would bump down the rutted trail with someone else trying to deposit another child at the orphanage.

The couple would stop their packing long enough to see whether the criteria were being met by this new applicant. (Somewhere along the line they had interviewed the director of a Brazilian orphanage who had declared you should never incorporate older children into a home because they bring established bad habits with them which are apt to disrupt any tranquility you might have been able to forge.) With this formula operative, any new boys had to be younger than seven and any new girls had to be under four. In retrospect, I guess I should be eternally grateful for this rule because during the next two months they could only find five children that both had birth certificates and met the age requisites!

This, of course, is hindsight. At the time I was the not-too-happy observer, the disinterested—but faultfinding—bystander. It seemed as though an absurd amount of stupidity was going down, but it surely wasn't any of my business—I wasn't on the Mission Committee. No one paid much attention, even though the mission president did look grieved every time I reiterated my warning that God was not going to let "you" get away with abandoning all these children.

At 23, I was so young. I considered myself more academic than domestic, and would be the last person, had I been on the committee, to suggest as the one to solve this problem. But since I wasn't on the committee I didn't hear the speculations about the advantages of keeping me so occupied. I had always been considered "high energy" and since I had no specific mission assignment to fill, I was supposed to spend most of my time studying Portuguese. As soon as the new school year started, George and I were planning to go to the missionary language school in Campinas for a year's study. Ever competitive, I knew if I studied hard I could get into an advanced class.

In the midst of all these departures, my father announced cheerfully the incredulous—to me—news that George had just been appointed the new manager of our *fazenda*. (Little did I know that the only reason my dad didn't appoint him manager of the second farm also was that he didn't have the courage to dislodge the managers who had been there several years already and who had no intentions of moving over for a young whippersnapper.) When I expressed grave misgivings about the wisdom of putting someone with limited language abilities and no farm experience in such a post, my dad said he had every confidence that George would learn quickly and do a great job. I wasn't as sure, but I had little time to think about it for almost immediately the suggestion was made that since no one had shown up willing to continue the orphanage work, why didn't George and I think about adopting them instead.

It was the craziest idea I'd ever heard. I now suspect my father and George were trying to keep me barefoot and out of their hair—all in one fell swoop. It also dawned on me, after the fact, that the only plausible reason this older couple had added five more children to the orphanage just before they headed over the horizon was for photo ops. It would have looked silly going back to the States with pictures of themselves and three small children in front of a building that was supposed to house 24 orphans. Anyone can raise three children! Most Americans in those days did. At least with eight, it appeared like more of a challenge—the start of an "important" Christian project—with appropriate slides to show to their Sunday school class back home.

What always amazed me is that never again in all the years which followed when I was raising these children did that couple ever contact us or them. No letter, no Christmas card, no birthday greetings, no requests for pictures, no presents, no funds. Out of sight, out of mind. But at this point I was still blissfully unaware. All I knew is that I had asked God to clear out those who didn't have a mission vision and I got left raising the kids.

A couple of weeks before this momentous decision, George and I had moved out of my parents' not-too-peaceful abode into a house across the path that had been vacated by one of those prayed-out émigrés. We invited a young Brazilian couple to share the space with us so we could learn Portuguese faster. It was a little primitive, but we were getting along nicely with the outhouse and the lean-to which had been added off the back porch for showers. (You heated water on the butane-tank stove and filled a galvanized bucket that had a showerhead welded on the bottom. Then you raised this contraption with a rope strung through a pulley on the roof beam high enough so you could stand underneath, regulate the water flow with a little lever and perform your ablutions before the bucket ran dry. The shower had a slat floor so the slop ran through the slats into a channel that dumped it all into the bushes behind the house. Since you could only use one bucket at a time, the runoff was never a worrisome amount. After a visiting American got conked unconscious when the filled bucket dropped on him, I always double-checked the knot on the cleat carefully when I raised the water bucket for my showers.)

In our new digs, to accommodate the Brazilian palate of the other couple, we ate beans and rice twice daily, lived close to nature and tried to read by kerosene lanterns at night—while keeping the mosquitos, no-see-ums and chiggers at bay. It was arduous but I was coping—until that fateful morning when George returned from a Mission Committee meeting to announce, "You know there are a lot of families that have eight children."

Still not getting it, I asked, "That's apropos of what?"

When it finally sank in that they were wanting me to adopt the children, I had no idea even where to begin. I'd seen the children in church, but I'd never really spoken to any of them—they didn't speak English and I knew very little Portuguese. The next two weeks sped by. I kept thinking someone would show up at the last minute to rescue me, but instead, two days after my 24th birthday, I found myself the mother of eight. The baby was two weeks shy of her second birthday and the oldest girl was now nine with everyone stair-stepping in between—girls that were three and five, and boys that were four, six, seven and eight.

So began one of the wildest prayer journeys of my life. In fact it was like a crash Ph.D. course on intercession because that is what we lived on—prayer. I was idealistic and had so many lessons to learn. I did remember that Paul admonished Timothy, "Despise not your youth" (1 Tm 4:12). In accepting this challenge I knew I needed divine intervention. Soon I had established a procedure that I have observed ever since. Each morning I would get up at 5:30, have a cup of tea and then spend an hour in Scripture reading and prayer. I also told the kids they were not allowed out of bed until 6:30 so I was assured a quiet hour before the stirrings of the morning began.

Daily I would try to read four chapters in the Bible—one each from the historical books and the prophetic books of the Old Testament and the gospels and the epistles in the New. It was during this hour that I brought the Lord my problems and needs, my wants and my dreams. After going over the day's anticipated activities, asking the Lord's blessings, I would pray for the children, my problems and concerns, trying to center my day, asking for divine intervention where needed. Then I would try to quiet my soul and listen to that still, small voice of the Spirit.

These were very creative hours for I felt that God was interacting with me, reminding me, directing me, prodding me, guiding me. The Bible reading was also a great source of inspiration for so often I would read a verse that was directly applicable to some situation I was facing. Of course the immediate necessity that drove me to my knees was figuring out how to access God's provision. It wasn't just trying to feed ten mouths that I had to worry about. We were surrounded by people living at the margins of subsistence. Because we had so much "stuff" they perceived us as wealthy—and themselves as worthy recipients.

Down through the years I've met some amazing saints. And then some not, too. But one thing I have noted is that no one is all good nor is anyone all bad. So it was I learned a vital prayer lesson from Helen, the woman who had started the orphanage (whose sins of omission and commission I could recount for hours). In spite of her obvious weaknesses, Helen was a very generous woman—that's what motivated her to take care of these orphans in the first place. She explained to me once that she tried to take seriously Christ's command to "give to everyone who asks." Thus, when Brazilians showed up at her door seeking handouts, Helen always gave.

This kind of word scurried about the jungle telegraph faster than the speed of light—imagine! an American with compassion! Daily the requesters thronged to her door and Helen dispensed powdered milk, sugar, rice, salt, beans, manioc flour, lard, cookies—anything to help these poor, struggling peasants keep body and soul together. When the load of provisioning all these people felt unbearable and she was finding it difficult to keep enough stocks on hand to feed the orphans, Helen stumbled on the verse in Psalms that says you guard your gates in vain unless the Lord guard them for you (127:1). Taking this seriously, she asked God to guard her gates so she would know that anyone who got through to her back door to ask for food, she was supposed to help.

There was no physical fence around the orphanage, let alone a gate, but that day the deluge stopped. Without saying a word or complaining to anyone, Helen found that people quit asking, so she didn't have to turn them away empty-handed. I heard this story from her as she was leaving because she thought the supplicants might return—but they didn't. I did feel this was a worthy precept and ever since I have tried to model my life on it, daily asking the Lord to guard my gates. Thus whoever gets "through" my gates I assume God has sent for a purpose and I try to attend to whatever needs they bring. This means you can't complain about being too busy when someone comes asking for assistance. Rather, you turn to the Lord and say, "Please help me with this one. I'm feeling beleaguered." Or when someone unexpectedly shows up at meal time, you don't have to complain, you just have to ask God to help the food go around—or else ask for inspiration for a creative alternative you can add to the pot which will quickly swell the contents to an appropriate amount.

This has happened to me so many times that I know it works. Countless people have sat at my table, eaten innumerable meals and the cruse of oil has never ceased to provide. I no longer worry about food. Having put this whole matter in God's hands I know that when extra mouths are going to appear without warning, I will have made too much or someone won't be as hungry as you expected or there is something in the cupboard to add the perfect complement to what's already going on the table. Long ago I decided that God does care about hospitality. Just as Jesus fed the multitudes and turned the water into wine, our obligation as followers of Christ is to say to the hungry who show up at our gates, "Come and dine."

But I didn't know this when I first started out. Though it was a bit rough at times, I have never regretted that those eight children got through my gates. The years devoted to raising them—plus the two of my own I later added to the menagerie—turned out to be a lot of fun. And whales of experience. Who else by age 39 had parented over 100 years of children? In the beginning the sustenance hurdle was the hard one. I was stuck here for a long time, trying to believe Jesus was right—we don't live by bread alone. This issue was a constant nag and kept me devoted to my prayer life for years as I tried hard to figure out how to keep food on the table on our $50-a-month allowance.

Housing was provided and there were no utility bills because there were no utilities—we bought 20 liters of kerosene with our groceries for the lamps and the rather ingenious refrigerator which managed to keep food almost cold from a heat-transfer system that operated on a larger version of a kerosene lamp. Since we were adopting the eight children instead of running an orphanage, no one said anything about increasing our stipend. Everyone got the same amount, regardless of how many children you had, so I assumed that meant we were supposed to stay within the $50 budget. Thus I found myself trying to feed *and* clothe eight still small, but growing, children plus us on this meager allowance.

One of the harsher elements in the transfer of these children to our care was that Helen was totally unhappy about turning them over to me. She wanted someone older, wiser and more domesticated to step into the gap, (but naturally the older and wiser knew better!). So to unfacilitate the process and show her ire, before she left, Helen managed to give away all the supplies, most of the collected children's clothing plus much of the kitchen equipment that had been donated for the orphanage. After all, I wasn't going to be running an orphanage, so I had no right to these accoutrements, Helen felt. I don't know why her favored Brazilian friends had more needs for all this, but when I came on the scene there was no fluff left anywhere in the system.

The entire transition consisted of one invited tour through the house—though I lived just across the path, it was my first time inside—the afternoon before they left so Helen could describe the children's schedule. I used to baby-sit for people who spent more energy clarifying my responsibilities for an evening to me than she did. After we waved them off down the jungle trail early one morning as they headed to the airport, I entered an almost-empty kitchen to make hot cereal for the first time in my life. There was enough oatmeal for a couple of mornings, but even oatmeal turned out to be a luxury beyond our budget.

Soon we were on a steady diet of cornmeal mush each morning. For lunch we had popcorn (Helen had assured me the children really liked this!) and then we had an early supper—our only real meal of the day and all we could afford on our budget—of rice, beans, cabbage salad plus a chicken plucked off the hoof every afternoon (a job I never was willing to do). Helen had also asserted that since the American palate was different from the Brazilian, she cooked two meals—one for the children which they ate at a small table with specially-made little chairs—and one for the adults served at a regular table. This I would not do! After all, this was no orphanage, these were our kids so we sat them at our table and they ate what we ate.

Recently we were visiting with Vera Lúcia, who was then five. Having raised ten, I can assure you that some kids turn out gooder than others. Of my litter, Vera was the goodest. She's no angel, but from the time she was little, her radiating smile and willingness to pitch in and go the second mile made her the moral lodestar of the family. During family discussions when schedule changes and new school timetables meant we needed to reassign duties, Vera's suggestion carried double weight because she would always do twice as much as what she'd expect of others. On this visit, as always when we get together, we began reminiscing about the early days. Since she was so young when Helen and her husband left, I thought Vera might have forgotten (I know most of the boys have only vague memories of anything other than the time they spent playing outdoors and the scrapes they got into—or almost got into). But Vera had that menu down pat. She remembered clearly those lean times.

I'm sure it marked all of us and I feel bad about how long it took me to figure out that I didn't have to buy into the system. God never said that all we could ask for was the minimum, but I was so young! I assumed that since I was asking for God's supernatural provision, I had to keep everything as miserly as possible. I admitted the lilies were allowed rather extravagant dress, but my worries nagged. What if the Lord provided generously so we could eat three meals today? How would I know whether God would get so unhappy with some overindulgence or infraction that we all might be put on bread-and-water for days to pay for an exorbitance or a crime?

Of course I didn't actually articulate such inanities, but I acted as if the ravens who flew in supplies today might go elsewhere tomorrow. Gradually I saw too many miracles not to put into practice the precept that "according to your faith be it unto you" and trust that the God who was putting food on the table today, would do it again tomorrow—and tomorrow—and tomorrow—and .... It was also years before I realized that God was willing to put lobster on our plates if I wanted it, not just those free-range chickens we ate daily. God is never a miser—one look at creation is enough to prove that— so if there is miserliness going down, it's not coming from the Lord who created stars without number and awesome beaches to contain the countless sands of the seas.

Never being a good one to dissemble, I finally got upset enough about our penurious life-style to complain to my father. Of course these were lean times for everyone. The mission had a lot of farm expenses and payroll costs and—as my father often pointed out—he had had nothing to do with starting the orphanage and so he didn't feel as though it were his "burden." Still, it would seem that just the normal milk of human kindness would be flowing enough to make my folks or someone see our plight and offer to help out. But they didn't—generosity and kindness have often been in short supply around missionary communities, I've discovered.

One day a couple living on our other farm came to visit bringing us a can of Argentine peaches—at almost a dollar a can, an unthinkable extravagance for us. My first reaction was: "A dollar would buy a lot of beans and rice. Why such a frivolous luxury item?" But I accepted it as graciously as I could and told the Lord how unhappy I was. The annoyance over that can of peaches burrowed so deeply into me that finally I cornered my dad with a 20-minute discourse prepared to explain why I thought we should have more of a monthly allowance— after all, I was trying to feed ten people for what he and Mom had for two, etc., etc., etc. Before I had finished the preamble, he had acquiesced, saying, "Sure, Faith, how much do you want?"

I was so taken back by his immediate compliance that I didn't have an answer prepared. I suggested the first number that came to mind, "What about $75 a month?"

"That's fine," he nodded sweetly.

It was so easy! And we had suffered for months! I was indignant and awestruck at all the Americans living around who watched us struggle without trying to help out or even give advice. But when I mulled it over during my morning devotions, I realized that it had been pride that had kept me from asking. I had wanted my dad or others to offer. Or maybe God should send down manna from heaven just because we were obviously in such distress—and I was being so good.

Instead, dealing with the mission was just like prayer: I had to learn to say "please" and "thank you." It was a good lesson—that I have to keep relearning—because we can't take God for granted any more than we can take our earthly support system for granted. When we need things, we have to go to the Lord in prayer and let our request be made known. Or go to the person who can obviously help you out and ask specifically.

Little by little I was empowered to begin taking charge of our situation. Dry milk was unbelievably expensive, so we had been buying fresh milk from Polish neighbors down the road. Every day we sent someone off on horseback with the homemade saddlebags designed to hold six empty *cachaça* (the local cane-sugar rum) liter bottles. I don't know where the rum bottles came from. Everyone around me claimed not to drink, but the empty bottles never seemed to be in short supply. While we watched (to prove it wasn't watered down) our neighbor would deftly funnel the still-warm milk from a gallon jug which she would swirl quickly to set up a centrifugal force so the milk would cling to the outside of the jug creating a natural air passage up the middle so it wouldn't glug-glug-glug slowly into our bottles. She would then seal each bottle tightly with a cork for the return trip and woe to the careless milk fetcher who bounced home too quickly and upended this arrangement. Even though no benefit derives from crying over spilt milk, I always felt better for having given a tongue-lashing to the slapdash soul.

This system wasn't flawless. Sometimes the cows were off their cycle and our supply was cut or bad weather would make it a trial to get the milk home. Finally it dawned on me that the God who owned the cattle on a thousand hills might be willing to give us our own cows if I asked for them. I wanted our children to have plenty of milk, so why not? When I prayed about it the next day during my devotions, it came to me that if I was really trusting God to supply all my needs according to the Lord's riches in Christ Jesus (Ph 4:19), I would be willing to scrap our budget and plunder our savings account (with all that insurance money—which I was hoarding for a rainy day and/or a trip back to the States). Besides there were almost four years left until the normal furlough time came around, so why worry? Anything could happen in that time.

Soon we were the proud owners of ten young heifers who were ready to start producing. Then it wasn't long before we had a 20-quart milk can delivered to the house every morning from our own pasture which provided a surfeit of milk for our household. From this point on I slowly figured out that God doesn't like me to have savings accounts. The Lord prefers to be my cushion, my disaster relief and my provision. Without fail, ever since, whenever I've attempted to get a savings account going, some emergency has come along to exhaust it almost immediately. Now I don't bother to try. Who needs emergencies?

But to cope with so much milk we all had to develop new skills. Graciano, now a bright five-year-old, got the job of standing on a chair by the stove so he could reach the big stainless steel pot and stir the milk. He was too small to lift the filled pan, but he was always careful to call someone as soon as the thermometer showed the milk had reached 178°, the quick pasteurization point recommended by some farming book we had. To avoid acquiring a cooked taste the milk was then set promptly in cool water in our cement laundry tank with its washboard sides. Later, about half was transferred to our kerosene-run refrigerator for drinking, while half was put in a cheese pot on the back of the wood-burning stove (we now had two stoves, one that used expensive butane tanks for quick cooking projects and the other that had to be stoked all day with wood—which was free for the gathering from the nearby cleared jungles).

So it went. Little-by-little I was asking the Lord for this or that. And God was awesomely gracious in providing way beyond anything I could ask or think. We began receiving surplus equipment sent down from American farms that long before had electrified and automated those processes: a stainless steel milk separator with about a hundred moving parts which Graciano loved to assemble and disassemble (the only problem was he then got curious about taking apart every machine he could get his hands on and not everything could he reconstitute); a hand-cranked food blender (even with dire warnings Graci could not resist taking that one apart and it was never was quite the same after he tried to figure out what made it whirl); a butter churn with a no-nonsense glass jar and paddles (with nothing for

Graci to dismantle but which an American neighbor later borrowed and promptly broke).

Self-taught, I nevertheless became adept at making butter and different kinds of cheeses and other dairy derivatives which supplemented our diet nicely—since I still believed that frugality was the path to godliness for me and couldn't bring myself to spend hard cash for such items. As our herd grew we soon had enough of these dairy products to supply not only my parents but neighboring missionaries with delicious, homemade butter and cheese.

Our life-style began improving in spite of that belief system buried deeply in my bones that if you were serving God you had to get by on the minimum. I noted a few anomalies. First, you could exempt flowers and plants because God made them and the tropical lushness produced exquisite varieties which sparkled up our unpainted home (God didn't produce paint directly). After the butter and cheese and fruits of the vine started enhancing our menus it began to dawn on me that instead of the bare bones I was taught to expect, my experience was teaching me just the opposite—the more you asked God for, the more you got—pressed down, shaken together and running over.

This came clearer the year we were the only missionaries left on the farm. My parents were on furlough in the States and the other couple had moved out to our other farm. Our financial situation was so precarious that when our pickup broke down and needed a $10 part for repair, we didn't have the funds to buy it. What to do? We finally negotiated a $100 loan at a nearby bank, but in order to sign the loan documents we had to ride the nine miles to town on horseback. Of course Brazil being Brazil there was some paperwork missing so we were asked to come back the next day to sign. My seat was so sore from the 18-mile ride that the next day we went to town on a horse-and-cart arrangement which wasn't that much more comfortable, but at least it hurt in new areas.

Coming home that day the question swirled in my head—why was I going through all this for a measly $100 which was so easy to come by in the States but required all this sweat and tears in the Brazilian economy? Without our eight children I would have left it all behind that day and headed north, but I knew with all the red tape involved it would be virtually impossible to get papers to take them to the States and then, once there, it would be enormously expensive to raise them. At least here on the farm we were producing a lot of our own food by now. Subsistence farming was my goal in life.

With all these money difficulties, I did try to figure out what the Lord was telling us. Then we had no more scraped our lives together with that $100 loan, when we got the dreadful news that the land company from which my parents and their friends and relatives had bought the two farms was in a legal foreclosure. The owner had died, the heirs were fighting in court and so a judge had preëmptorily ruled that all back payments had to be made in 30 days or land would be subject to confiscation. While the court battle had been going, on no one had collected land payments, so we were now in arrears $4,000—which seemed a colossal sum from our vantage point. We only heard about this third-hand because our landowners' names had appeared on a published list in a newspaper in Curitiba—a thousand light-years away from where our heads were. It had taken a couple weeks for the news to reach us, and now there were only 15 days left before we were in default. It would take two weeks to get a letter to the States. Besides, my parents were traveling and I knew not where they were laying their heads.

It seemed an insurmountable obstacle. The bank hadn't wanted to give us $100 because the loan wasn't secured by land—everyone knew about the land company's imbroglio because everyone in the area had bought their land from the same developers. What would happen if we lost the land? There was nothing else to do but fling ourselves on the Lord. It seemed so impossible, but, as they say, if all else fails, try God.

What a miraculous answer to prayer it was! We had missionary neighbors who never seemed to have any more money than we did but who had heard about the land developer's court problems. They came to visit. Not knowing how much we needed to come up with, they admitted they came by specifically to tell us that they had just received a $4,000 donation for a project that wasn't going to get underway for another nine months. If it would help, they would be willing to lend us that $4,000 for nine months.

If it would help! Again it was penny-perfect assistance. Who else to thank but the Lord for once more providing our needs in such astounding ways? And just as the nine months was up, my parents, who by now had been apprised of the situation, raised the needed funds in the States so we could repay our benefactors on time.

In my devotions when I prayed about all this, I realized that when I asked for $100, I got $100, when I asked for $4,000, I got $4,000. It was a watershed experience. My days of miserliness were not behind me, but they were ebbing. I had been too carefully taught by my missionary world ever to become extravagant, but at least I knew my God was not a miser. My trust level might be faulty, but the Lord was willing to supply our needs way beyond anything I could ask or expect.

In the following years my trust in God's promises grew so much that I now bordered on the outrageous. After we had been in Brazil for eight years someone on the Mission Committee (I was now allowed to attend because I was handling all the farm payroll and books, the mission office work and doing the year-end accounting) was lamenting the dearth of good literature available in Portuguese. I suggested that we start a publishing venture ourselves—after all, other missions in Brazil were doing it—and it was a nice way to spread our ministry around the country. Everyone else demurred, saying that with their busy schedules it was unrealistic. Something inside made me persist with the idea until someone finally suggested that if I thought it was a viable ministry, why didn't I organize it?

So the little red hen did just that. When I prayed asking God for guidance, I felt I was being given a green light. By this time Neny, the original baby, was already nine, and I had four teenagers in the house—plus my own babies who were now four and five. Everyone was in school for at least part of the day and many hands make light work—so we had a household that was humming along smoothly. One more project wouldn't be that difficult, I decided, so that's how it happened that I founded a small mission publishing house right out there in the jungles.

Missionary friends who were godparents to my youngest had left our area for the bright lights of São Paulo to work with a religious publishing operation there. Because of them I had met the rest of their team and so when this idea emerged, I talked this group into helping me with the project: I would raise the money, choose the title, get the Portuguese rights, then arrange for a translator and proofreader. They would use their typesetter and graphic design person to produce the book and distribute it through their channels, keeping 50 per cent of the income for their efforts, putting the other 50 per cent into a fund that I would use to publish another book. It was a pretty slick system. No overhead to speak of. Everything generated was plowed back into the project. The mission gave me $1,500 seed money and soon I had all the burners cooking.

In the process I agreed to help some German Lutheran religious sisters publish their materials in Brazil. Someone had given me a couple pieces of their literature and I had been most impressed by their story because it reminded me a bit of what I'd been through. Originally they had come together after a horrendous bombing raid on their town at the end of World War II. There was scarcely any food in the land, and their town was reduced to rubble, so of necessity they began to pray and trust God to provide for their needs. In fact, they decided then they would eat only food which they grew themselves or which was donated to their cause. Any gifts given them as cash would be used for building materials and outreach mission programs.

God heard their prayers and abundantly provided them with food, wondrously supplying their needs. In humility they adopted the garb of medieval nuns, took vows of chastity and poverty and committed themselves to obey a spiritual rule based on that of St. Francis expanded a bit—but this was Germany, not Italy, and they were Protestants, not Catholics. In the 13th century, using a form of bibliomancy, Francis had derived his spiritual rule by opening the Gospels at random to find three postulates: 1. "If you would be perfect, go, sell what you possess and give to the poor, and you will have treasure in heaven; and come, follow me" (Mt 19:21); 2. "Take nothing for your journey, no staff, nor bag, nor bread, nor money" (Lk 9:3); and finally 3. "If anyone would come after me, let them deny themselves and take up their cross daily and follow me" (Lk 9:23). Even though Francis was adamant that this rule was God-given and suitable for the multitudes that thronged to follow his example, Rome found the original Rule of St. Francis a bit simplistic and later advocated some modifications in keeping with the changing times.

These German Lutherans, seven centuries later, adapted Francis's rule so daily they pray for their bread. The God who sees the most insignificant sparrow falter in flight never fails them. They have kept up the routine year in and year out for 50 years. God is their sustainer and providence. Without supernatural intervention they do not eat, so daily the original group of 25 plus the hundred new recruits have plenty of motivation to ask God earnestly for their food.

They had learned the same lesson I had: God, the owner of the cattle on a thousand hills, obviously knew about my shortages and could easily have diverted one or two critters our way and allowed us to feast daily on the finest edibles around. Since we didn't—until I had learned to be very specific and present God with an itemized list which was filled to the letter too many times to think it accidental—there had to be an important lesson here. It seemed obvious that God was more interested in my learning to pray and trust the Lord to provide than in our eating. We never starved, but until I grasped that I was supposed to concentrate on being specific and saying "please" and "thank you," we didn't do all that well either. Even after I had the food-prayer down pat and we were eating well, still all my troubles had not disappeared.

Then I realized: this was kindergarten. God got my attention by making me responsible for putting food in all those mouths. When that was organized, it was time to move on to other areas.

I began praying for an ever-widening circle of concerns: The kids. Their health. Their schooling. The farm. Our payroll. Our workers. The neighbors. The office. The mission community. My writing career. Relatives. A publishing house! It was wild. The more I trusted God, the more God proved to be trustworthy. Why God wanted to be our provision, I could not understand. But being a pragmatist, I knew that prayer worked and I wasn't going to give it up. Even though some thought I was presumptuous for bothering God with such inconsequential predicaments, they soon had to admit that it did appear that God was, indeed, answering these prayers in ways no one could humanly explain.

Which brings us to a third principle of prayer: *God cannot be taken for granted as an amorphous source of goodwill.* Just because something would be nice to have, we cannot expect God to read our minds and automatically provide it for us. We must ask, specifically, according to the Lord's riches in Christ Jesus for what we need and what we want.

One joyous boon in all this learning to pray is that I've raised ten children who know beyond a shadow of a doubt there is an immanent God who answers prayers. So the chain goes on—the truths we have learned from the prophets of old about God's provisions we pass on to the next generation so that these insights, way beyond our understanding, might continue to be spread abroad, far and wide. This is not a message that should be hid under a bushel or kept private—it is good news for all who have ears to hear and hearts to understand.

PRAYER FOR GOD'S PROVISION

Compassionate God, You have always proved your willingness to hear us when we come to you in need. Just as you provided daily manna and garments that would not wear out to the children of Israel in the wilderness, so we acknowledge that you are willing to supply all our needs according to your riches in glory by Christ Jesus. We ask that you might again in your graciousness grant us our desires. Make us worthy recipients of your goodness and help us use the gifts we receive from you in ways that are pleasing to you. Open our hearts to you and free us from all anxiety, through Christ our Lord. Amen.

4.

God's Choreography

"Do not put the Lord your God to the test."

(Mt 4:7)

Anyone who has spent much time in Los Angeles hurtling along the freeways and byways of this city either believes in guardian angels or doesn't think about it. Most who contemplate the road would acknowledge that the sudden jerk of a driver's wrist, a reckless attempt to cut in or an unpropitious mechanical failure is all that is needed to catapult you into sudden vehicular mayhem.

Not even luck seems to stretch far enough to explain why calamity doesn't strike more often. Californians tend to be mocked because so many new religions are started underneath these palm trees, but it has occurred to me that driving these highways tends to make a believer of you. Someone, somewhere is watching over the incredible choreography that is needed to keep you from slamming into that reckless teenage driver who doesn't stop at the stop sign or mowing down that feckless matron who doesn't look before she steps out in the street from behind parked cars or piling up behind the truck driver who has just jackknifed across three lanes of traffic to keep from slamming into the guy who cut in front of him. As you swerve out of disaster's trajectory or screech by with inches to spare, you thank your lucky stars, your guardian angels or mere providence.

Guardian angels are scriptural. Interestingly, Satan used them, quoting the promises of the Psalms in his second temptation of Jesus. Having figured out with the first temptation he couldn't get Jesus to start worrying about where he was going to get his next meal, the devil decided to try another tactic and see if he could trip him up through rash presumption and effrontery at his role in life. After taking him to the pinnacle of the temple, Satan challenged Jesus, "If you are the Son of God, . . . throw yourself down. For it is written: 'He will command his angels concerning you, and they will lift you up in their hands, so that you will not strike your foot against a stone'" (from Ps 91:11-12). Sounds reasonable. Show the world your power. Let those scoffing Pharisees check out your authority base once and for all. It's biblical. Did God not say it?

Ignoring the taunt, Jesus didn't fall for that one either. Instead Jesus quoted scriptures back at Satan: "Do not put the Lord your God to the test" (from Dt 6:16). Basically he said he would trust in God's planning and not try to inject his own strategy on the scene. After all, it was the Spirit who had led Jesus into the desert. As the "Son of God" he was willing to trust God to send food or ministering angels when the time was right—not lash out at his lot in life.

So often, like Jesus, as soon as we've passed the smallest entry level quiz about trusting God for bread and our material sustenance, it dawns on us that there is a new lesson on the horizon—God's choreography. Our history is in God's hands. If we find ourselves on the pinnacle of the temple, we must not be foolhardy and decide this is a time to prove to everyone what spiritual power we have. This is the time to hunker down and trust.

My moment of epiphany came one summer morning at my alma mater—some seven years after I'd adopted the children. Patience is wonderful. No matter how difficult it is to believe during a two a.m. feeding, children do grow up. And in our family, with everyone developing and becoming more competent, I soon found I was not as anchored to the house as I had been. We still had a busy household, but the chores were shared and I could get away if need be. I was back in the States for a few weeks because miraculously I had been given a trip so I could go to a family reunion. It was to be held at a rented lakeside Bible camp in rural Wisconsin—the only place large enough to accommodate our burgeoning "Sandpile"—but a long haul for just a weekend escapade so I decided to take advantage of the vacation and also attend a writing seminar. With a couple weeks lag time in between the two events, I noted that it "just happened" the interval coincided with a summer session at my old college which alumni could attend free.

To avoid dorm living I called an old college friend who was getting a master's at Northwestern, asking if I could stay with her. She picked me up at the airport in a sporty convertible and soon we were in the bowels of Chicago—grimy, slovenly and vaguely menacing. Her basement apartment didn't remind me a whit of the dorms: no direct sunlight filtered in through half-buried windows; the heavy damask curtains, candles and incense made it seem even gloomier. Walls and doors were decorated with protest signs and suggestive posters which I tried not to examine too closely. She was living with her husband, also a classmate, but neither felt marital fidelity was necessarily a priority.

A time warp had developed during the years I'd been living out of the country—my classmates had obviously been foraging in fields I had never thought of. Not wanting to be critical, I still was saddened; they were repudiating everything we had been taught to believe. It soon became evident that no one cared much about my tropical sojourn. The tropics capturing everyone's attention involved real life-and-death issues in Vietnam. The war was in full swing—and our generation had turned out to be the fall guys. Pondering what they were dying for and why we were involved led to a general questioning of all authority. With limb at risk and extinction so imminent, conventional values were easily disavowed. Campus unrest spilled over into the society at large and the Broadway musical *Hair* was thumbing its stage nose at our social mores. Changes everywhere kept me reeling. What to think? Who was right? Where was our country headed? Why had God let all this happen?

The first day I messed up on the suburban train schedule so my friend dropped me at our alma mater in time for registration. The morning sun was sparkling the dewy earth as she drove off without stopping. Later she told me this had been her first return to the campus since graduation and simply seeing the old haunts had made her feel nauseous. It was just too perfect—safeguarded and sheltered from all the world's rankness: the newly mowed green lawns bordered with bright summer flowers primly squaring off the brick buildings; the tall trees shading the measured movement of the kempt academic community sauntering along its tranquil walks. This no longer reflected the reality of where my classmates were living.

Even the linoleum in the administration building had the same familiar worn spots. Amazingly, while the world outside was erupting and everyone I knew was pushing the boundaries and jettisoning traditions, here all went on undisturbed, comfortable, serene. Or almost. The journalism course that had enticed me back to school was canceled—the professor backed out at the last moment. I was established in Chicago for two weeks with people whose life-style I found disquieting but with nowhere else to go. So I made the best of it and switched my registration to a class on Christian mythology given by a professor I'd heard was good but whom I'd never had—a slight course alteration which managed to change my life forever.

We read nine books in ten days—three by C.S. Lewis, two by Tolkien and Charles Williams and one by George MacDonald and Dorothy Sayers—a truly wondrous assignment. I thought I'd died and gone to heaven. No kids, no cooking, no responsibilities and I was "forced" to read a book a day. Our four-hour class ended at noon and then I would hunker down in the air-conditioned library to float off into one mythical land after another. Our small class of 17 students was a magical mix of people from around the world. The last day the professor admitted that in 38 years of teaching he'd never had a class to equal ours. The enchantment in the books we were reading seemed to filter into the air around us.

One morning, after an all-night rain had scrubbed the skies clean leaving each green leaf glimmering, we settled into our accustomed slots. The professor turned from watching a squirrel scampering up an old oak and prefaced his prayer with which he opened every class by musing on the lovely morning scene. Then he added, "You know, if God isn't in *every* moment of your life, God isn't in *any* moment of your life."

I was stunned. Every moment? Surely not? For seven years as I struggled raising our large family in the midst of the tropical heat and the spiders, the outhouses and the fleas, the discomfort and the exhaustion, battling myriad elements to keep our family afloat, my underlying rant at God had been, "Whatever did I do to deserve all this?" Now Dr. K. was saying that this was not a mistake, a foul-up, an error in someone's judgment. This history I'd been living through was God's moment for me. I wasn't the victim of other people's stupidity, I was *chosen*. I had been standing on the pinnacle of my life's temple and all I had wanted to do was jump.

Suddenly with this new spin on my life, it seemed as if the Lord was saying, "Why couldn't you trust me? Don't you think I knew what I was doing? You wanted to be a writer? I was trying to help you out by telescoping a few of life's experiences for you. You should be thankful. How many other 32-year-olds have had your preparation? Or lived almost a decade without electricity, telephones or TV on one of the world's vanishing frontiers? Or ...? Or ...? Or ...?"

I was being given an enormous opportunity to acquire instruction and wisdom and all I did was complain. As a youngster reading Bible stories, I would shake my head in sheer stupefaction at how the children of Israel could put so much energy into murmuring. Why in the world were they so dumb? Couldn't they understand what God was saying with all those miracles? Had they lost their minds? Their memories? Look at all the manna—every day. Look at the pillar of fire each night and the daily cloud covering! Look at the shoes that never wore out and the clothes that lasted for 40 years. What were they thinking of? Like Peter I was convinced others might stumble, but I'd never fall into such a trap.

When it dawned on me that all my sniveling and feeling sorry for the heavy burden I was forced to shoulder was tantamount to that wilderness murmuring, I was overwhelmed. Here for seven years I had been living a miracle—feeding, clothing and educating a dozen people, first on $50 and then $75 a month. The supernatural answers to my prayers for sustenance were so numerous—and routine—that it emboldened me to branch out to what some considered to be immoderate requests—like the new publishing venture.

I'd even prayed for this second trip to the States in eight years (a restrained missionary only went once every five years). I justified my request by pointing out that I had gone through hardships others hadn't faced. When Heidi was a baby I'd not even seen asphalt for two years. With the closest paved road still a twelve-hour drive away, I'd discovered that the two babies and eight children made me functionally irreplaceable. Now I was claiming this second trip as God's payback for being such a faithful steward. (As if bright city lights are due recompense for devoted service!)

This trip I knew was a miracle. Every five years the Sand family reunions were held because my parents and my aunt and uncle, missionaries in Africa, coördinated their furloughs so the entire family could come together for a time of reconnecting, playing, praying and laughing over old stories. My father then had seven living siblings who over the years had produced 29 children, most of them married with families of their own. As I was about to miss the second reunion, I pointed out to my folks that since we scheduled our furloughs alternately with them, ipso facto, I would never get a chance to attend one of the reunions as long as I remained in Brazil.

This veiled threat prompted an unusual favor—a gift still incomprehensible. Most would not consider the source of this patronage—really matronage—remarkable, but for me it was phenomenal. Mother, having recently received a small legacy from her family, offered to pay for my trip out of these funds. The strangest part of the offer was that even though she lived across the path from me in Brazil, she never came near our house and really didn't like to be around me. She even proposed paying for the trip but then not attending the reunion herself so we wouldn't have to be together for a weekend. This wasn't altogether altruistic, because the spite she didn't reserve for me, she bequeathed on my father's family, but finally Papa convinced her that with over a hundred people being together for the gathering, she and I could probably coexist peaceably for that limited time—and there were some members of the family she did enjoy.

Looking back on all the years we were neighbors in Brazil I realize that during that entire period (and since) aside from that trip my mother never gave me another present which was appropriate or welcome. Her rancorous and malicious acts were interminable. When I finally left Brazil and got away from her pernicious attacks on everything I was and did, she disinherited me to make sure I got the message. So this gift trip to the family reunion was a peculiar deviation from her long-established pattern and I knew then and am convinced today that only God could have choreographed this unlikely miracle.

Like one of Tolkien's small turnings, this trip started me on a track that finally led me out of the jungles. During the years of raising the children, in spite of all the miraculous provisions I had been receiving in answer to my prayers, I had been putting the Lord my God to the test almost daily, complaining about my situation, grumping about my suffering, pointing out the injustice of how this one or that one treated me. So when Dr. K. made this pithy comment, it was a wake-up call. I knew I needed to get to the place where I could accept my lot in life. "Not my will, but thine be done," is a hard one, but repeatedly the words, *If God isn't in every moment of your life, God isn't in any moment of your life,* kept echoing in my head.

Curiously enough, years later when I mentioned to Dr. K. how special this statement had become to me, he not only did not remember saying it, I got the impression he didn't necessarily believe it. But by then it had become an unshakable foundation on which I stood. Whenever I began to doubt or pout or fret or protest, at the back of my mind something would trigger the line. I didn't always pay attention, but deep down I knew it was required of me to see God in every moment of my life. Whatever the trouble, I had to trust the Lord to work this one out, too, quieting my soul and trusting. Like Jesus, I had to quit trying to escape the plan that God had worked out for my life.

This simple phrase also helped me accept God's choreography of my life. Since I began each morning in my devotions dedicating my day to God, asking the Lord to design my way, conversely I knew that everything that happened had to be part of God's overall strategy. I didn't tell the Lord how to keep the stars in motion, so I should stop complaining about what seemed askew in my world.

The corollaries were obvious: no more fretting about missed telephone calls (no sweat in the unwired jungles, but a perennial problem when we were doing business in São Paulo where the system was atrocious), no more complaining about the too-frequently stolen mail (whatever went astray, you could leave to God who was in that moment, too), the bungled connections and the lost opportunities. If I were trying to call someone and kept getting a busy signal, or could not get a dial tone even to start the call, I'd stop and pray about it, asking the Lord to help me make connections if I was supposed to get through. A lot of times this happened immediately, but not always and then I would stop and listen. Maybe I wasn't supposed to contact this person. Or when something was preventing my carrying through on plans, instead of shoving and pushing and insisting, I'd again pray and try to get calm enough to hear what it was the Lord was saying through this incident.

It was incredible how this worked. After committing the day to God's watchkeeping, I would stand back and observe stunning scheduling unfold. The phone call I couldn't make, I discovered should not have been made. The stymied plan meant I was available for something even better. Some called it my charmed life. I knew it was merely a prayed-over life. Brazilians would shrug their shoulders and exclaim that I obviously was the goddaughter of Jesus Christ himself, even after I told them it was nothing unique to my position—all you had to do was say "please" and "thank you" to the God who was willing to do the same for all who came and asked.

Letting God choreograph your steps was especially effective with tedious Brazilian red tape. I once went to Rio to meet a ship bringing my parents and two other American couples who were coming to work on the *fazenda*. My folks wanted me to come help them through customs because between them they were bringing in five tons of "stuff." An old-timer once commented that you could predict the longevity of missionaries staying on the field in reverse proportion to the baggage they brought with them. This was true with the couple that had the most, because they stayed three months unpacking all their crates and decided when they were through that it was really too primitive for their taste, so having just finished settling in, they repacked and left, taking all their accoutrements of American living with them. Fortunately I was unaware of what was to come as I stood on the Rio docks welcoming them to Brazil.

A corollary to the truth that God is in every moment of your life is that you cannot spend a lot of energy on negative thoughts. So I went to Rio having prayed fervently, trusting these prayers would be effectual, availing much. It was common knowledge that everyone involved in the customshouse was corrupt. The wag had it that after working as a customs' official for three years, you could retire for life. I've always said that if the Brazilians in the military, the police and the government put as much ingenuity and energy into doing positive, constructive projects as they do in stealing and connivery the country would have no problems. This is not to say that the country isn't full of wonderful, honest people—they just never would stoop to work in an official government or police job because everyone knows the entire system is crooked.

With this in mind as I went to Rio, I insisted that no one in our group talk about these problems, think negatively or put any energy into pessimistic or cynical statements. Our God was more powerful than any customs' agent and all we needed to do was trust the Lord and expect God to intervene on our behalf. I was willing to handle the paperwork, but everyone else had to coöperate by praying and thinking positively about the entire operation.

The day after the ship arrived my folks and George took the newcomers on excursions to the various magnificent sites of Rio while I took Heather and Heidi, then six and seven, with me back down to the docks because it wasn't proper for me to be alone. Also someone had once told me that when you want officials to act on your behalf in Brazil, you should never sit down because with their inbuilt sense of chivalry, Brazilians are uncomfortable as long as you are standing and so are more apt to expedite your request. I went dressed to impress and planned to stand all day. It also wouldn't hurt, I figured, to have the girls with me since they were at a really cute stage and made friends with everyone who came near them.

After a few hours I was sent to get an absolutely necessary signature from another official across town—just as all the offices were closing for lunch. I prayed furiously and, sure enough, when I arrived the official (who only worked mornings) was inexplicably still in his office and I prevailed on him to give up his signature. At two, when the custom offices opened up again after lunch, I showed up at the docks with the signed papers and a cheery greeting. The woman at the desk nodded bleakly, nonplussed that I hadn't hit a roadblock. Several times she scowled at me and told me I should come back in a week to handle this more expeditiously, but I patiently explained that we lived too far away for that and so needed to get everything through customs immediately. Every time someone came near me, I would smile my sweetest, decline to sit down, and pray silently, thanking the Lord for choreographing this moment.

Finally, that evening as they were about to close the office, some official agreed that everything was in order and told an inspector who had been in and out all day to go release the crates. My father had fortunately appeared by then so he went to arrange for a truck because it seemed the baggage would be on the dock in an hour. Just as the stevedores were wheeling out the liberated baggage (with no bribe asked for or paid) a Baptist missionary walked up. He'd been coming down to this office almost daily for three months trying to get one of their missionary's household goods out of customs. He took in the huge pile of boxes, barrels and bags and inquired when this had first arrived. When I told him it had been in Rio for a little over a day, he frowned quizzically and asked how we had managed to get it out of customs so fast. I gave him my most saintly expression and said, "I just really believe in prayer and we've been praying about this a lot." He glowered at me in my mini-skirt and retreated without a word.

The first thing my mother had said to me years before when I'd arrived in Brazil and stepped out of the DC-3 onto the grassy runway in Umuarama, the little tropical town near our *fazenda*, was, "Now that you're in Brazil, Faith, you're going to have to wear longer skirts."

"It's great to see you, too, Mom," I replied.

Fashions were short and in my youth I couldn't see why coming to Brazil meant I had to look frumpy. So I hadn't changed my style, much to the chagrin of some in the missionary community who thought I needed to be more repressed. Then Brazil caught up with the rest of the world and everyone started wearing shorter skirts. But I never understood why missionaries would get so unhappy when the Lord answered my prayers in spite of the clothes I chose to wear. All I knew is that when I was dealing with officialdom I tried to look my best, treat them graciously, expecting them to do what was needed and then think as positively as possible while I kept praying silently throughout. Of course there were times I was so furious at the corruption and thievery that I'd lose it, but I knew if I could keep a positive attitude, fervent prayer did avail.

Certainly, throughout these years I was not without my problems or people in my life who mistreated me (in my view) or kept me from doing what I wanted to do. When that happened, at least in my head I knew that I needed to stop, get to a calm center and ask the Lord to take over. Though I might be justified in getting angry, I knew that when the Spirit of the Lord was operative in my life I would be able to love as I am loved. You also maintain your inward peace if you can let God fight your battles, handle the restitution and mete out judgment in the Lord's own time—not always the easiest thing for me to do.

King David had an interesting insight about those who do us wrong: "God will go before me and will let me gloat over those who slander me. But do not kill them, O Lord our shield, or my people will forget" (Ps 59:10-11). So David implies that without adversity, we would overlook the role God is playing in our lives. If everything went our way, we'd have no reason to ask for succor or remind the Lord of God's promises to us or even to pray for relief. And we certainly would have no opportunity to do good to the nasties in our life.

Another temptation is to pray for God's choreography and then start worrying. Of course, when I was in Brazil with our large household and all the comings and goings of scores of people, I could have spent 25 hours a day worrying about this and that. But I soon deduced that worrying did not one iota help. If I had 20 guests appearing for lunch, I would get upset if something untoward occurred to slow down my preparations as I scurried to get ten children reasonably cleaned and presentable plus the lunch made, the table set and flowers arranged.

In those days I wore my hair long and curled, so getting dressed always took more time. With my background ("A lady is never seen in public with curlers") I would start to panic if it seemed as though I was going to be caught in the kitchen still in my grubbies, with my hair up. Then I began to notice that no matter when people said they were going to show up (and with no telephone plus our miserable dirt roads, this was always a rough estimate, at best) they could be early, they could be late, but they always arrived just after I'd put the concluding touches on the meal and had run into my bedroom to get cleaned up. As soon as I'd finished combing out my hair, more times than I could count, you could hear the vehicle coming down the road.

Something seemed wrong about this. Sure, I had asked God to choreograph the day, but why did God care about my vanity? Wasn't I supposed to be mortifying my flesh the way they taught me in all my Christian boarding schools? It kept on happening so repeatedly I knew that it was more than a coincidence. Finally I accepted that the God who dressed the lilies of the field more splendiforously than King Solomon was able to adorn himself, cared because I cared. Not because it was vital to the kingdom, not because it was spiritual, just because I'd asked God to arrange my day and the Lord knew my hang-ups better than I did myself.

Subsequently when I extrapolated this to all those high school rules that seemed so silly and got me so many detentions, it occurred to me that my intuition was probably right. What was important to God was not necessarily what was important to the school administrators, and vice versa. The Lord didn't care about their regulations as much as they did. That's why God kept answering all my prayers for this and that even while I was disturbing their peace, piling up detentions and being made to memorize Bible verses on Saturday mornings. God wasn't pushing their petty rules because most of them were concerned with outward signs of piety, whitewashing a mean, harsh sepulchre. They tended to be like the ones to whom Jesus told the parable of the Pharisee and the tax collector: "People who thought they were better than others and who looked down on everyone else" (Lk 18:9).

The truly spiritual concerns, like putting all that scripture away in my memory bank so I would have it available to meditate on day and night when I would need it, were probably pleasing to the Lord, so you might deduce that God was happy even when I infringed their inconsequential regulations which "inspired" me to memorize scripture virtually each week. I do not find it surprising that the Saturday I learned how to cheat the system and wrote the verses out on eyesavers instead of memorizing them, it was changed to an hour of Saturday chores. At that point I was breaking a meaningful law—cheating—so then God stepped in and said, "Enough of this nonsense." Wearing pajamas in a snowstorm hardly paved the road to hell. (We did find the Saturday chores more onerous, so it gave us slight pause in pursuing the battle.)

One benefit of these scrapes was that I was not tempted to have an overblown notion of my own piety. Like the tax collector/publican, I was in a better position to go home forgiven than all those hypocrites who thought they were being Christlike because they obeyed all the orders from on high—while judging, condemning, criticizing and finding fault with us sinners in detention hall. A few years later I heard that the school's entire policy was revamped. Maybe our kicking against the pricks made the administration take notice.

Still the real problem in Christendom is how little emphasis is put on obeying the edicts that Christ mandated (love your enemies, do good to those who harm you, turn the other cheek, do not judge, do not resist evil, give to everyone who asks) in favor of the policies and principles that we forge to keep our world neat and orderly. Fascism hardly is compatible with Christianity. And there has never been anything prim and proper about the work of God's Spirit. Just as Saul was hurled to the ground and blinded on his way to Damascus to administer detentions to all those who were disobeying the edicts of the religious hierarchy, so when the Spirit gets hold of us we are shaken to our core, our priorities are scrambled—and our reputation is apt to suffer as well.

In looking back at my traumatizing school experiences, I could see that indeed God had been in those moments of my life just as I could see God in all subsequent moments. And ever since that bright summer morning at my alma mater I have clung to the fact that God is in every moment of my life. Period. Not always does it make sense, not always does it seem fair, not always does it make me happy, but over the years I slowly realized this was a God I could trust. I was part of the Lord's design. I wasn't abandoned. I wasn't here by chance. As C.S. Lewis said, I could only see the ragged back edge of the quilt with all its tangled knots and obscured pattern, but I could rest assured that from the Quilter's view it all worked out.

This also helped mitigate my worrying. As the children grew older and started spreading their wings, the tendency was to forget that I was to entrust them to God's care and watchkeeping—even if they were late or didn't show up for a meal or somehow escaped my purview. (Strange, but I find the nesting urge is so primordial that as long as they were under my roof, it was okay. They could be sick, obnoxious, cantankerous or feuding at home and I was fine—I might be shrilling at them, but that was to be expected. Once they headed down that trail, though, even if it was to a church meeting, a Bible camp or a "worthy" function, I had to go into overdrive on my prayers to keep from worrying.) Since we had no phones, there was no way to call home to justify the tardiness, the change in plans, the new ETA. There was nothing to do but trust. Maybe I gave up worrying because I had so many charges to worry about, but along the line I realized that what I needed to do was pray that my children's guardian angels would surround them and protect them from harm, danger and accident and then trust that if they were not protected from harm, danger and accident then that was part of God's quilt pattern and I wasn't supposed to interfere.

To this day when I face difficulties, I find it necessary to recite the old slogan, "If you worry, you don't trust and if you trust, you don't worry." I do not lead a worry-free existence, but I've certainly lessened my allotment. Not having reached perfection, I still have my anger, my miserliness, my judgments. Recently I agreed to host a Spanish student for a month. Heather came home unexpectedly for a weekend and after observing our Spaniard's behavior for an hour, she asked me whatever had made me say yes to this aggravation.

I don't know. Dementia? At the time I agreed it seemed this was to be a rare month when I would be home by myself. Since I had received such gracious hospitality from so many delightful Spaniards, I thought I could consider this payback time. For all my goodwill, I was assigned this perfectly lovely, totally selfish, rude and ungrateful 17-year old. I was irritated, furious and disapproving until I went to church on Sunday and heard the Gospel lesson about the Good Samaritan—the worthy infidel who had compassion. I was chagrined and left church asking God for compassion for this obviously wealthy kid with no manners.

The next morning during my devotions, the light went on! Of course, this is what I must look like to God: totally selfish, rude and ungrateful. Besides helping me keep my not-too-pious self in perspective (how can I love an enemy when I can't even love an insolent, thoughtless houseguest?), not only was God giving me a chance to understand what true love is all about, but I was allowed to get a glimpse of the overview. After all, the Lord doesn't love me because I am selfless, thoughtful and gracious, the Lord loves me because God is love. I have done nothing to "deserve" this love. God merely *is* love. That's God's nature. Love is who God is. So in this situation, aside from getting this insight into my own lack of love, I was being given the opportunity to go the second mile. (I managed maybe a block and a half before I deposited her back at the bus which would take her to the airport and went home singing the "Hallelujah Chorus.")

It also seemed that my exasperation derived from that fact that even though down deep I would like to be as selfish, rude and ungrateful as my guest, my training and background obligate me to obfuscate and mask what I think in order to be more socially acceptable. I did manage a few unpleasant asides and dour looks, but mostly I was all smiles because that is how we've been trained to respond. Of course we conveniently try to forget that while we were yet sinners, Christ died for us and even the pagans love those who are lovely. If the Spirit were truly operative in my life, I would let the mind of Christ be in me and love those who irritate me, who cheat me, who scoff at me and belittle me.

So in spite of my muddles and failures, this is how I've learned to walk with my God daily. Over the years in countless ways God has smoothed my schedules, coördinated my visitors, reminded me to do this, stock up on that, or plan ahead. When someone asks me how I accomplish so much in any given day, it seems too arrogant to say that it's God who keeps me centered and who intervenes on my behalf, but knowing I shouldn't take credit for someone else's work, I do try to divulge that I pray, asking God to plan my schedule each day and "It really works."

Since there are relatively few Spanish lasses who bluster into my life, I know that when they do, it's a wake-up call—a reminder of how far short I fall from the mark and how little aggravation it takes to have me back whining. Besides, since I continue to ask God to guard my gates, whenever anyone gets through the gate, I know there is some reason behind it, something either I need to give to this person or glean from this encounter.

I have discovered that asking God to choreograph your life is like the wilderness manna—it tends to be good only for about a day at a time. Maybe two if you're crossing the date line or there's some extenuating circumstances, but God wants us in a constant relationship. It is not a prayer when you go around thinking it would be nice if such-and-such would happen. Just because God could easily arrange thus-and-so for you, it does not necessarily follow that God *will* arrange it until you stop and pray, saying "please" and "thank you." God is into establishing a two-way communication system—a dance where the Lord is leading and you're following—God, the director; you, the performer.

Once while I was on a six-month sabbatical in Madrid living with some very fervent Christians, I casually mentioned to my gracious hosts that I had prayed for a parking space and gotten one right outside their apartment. They were horrified to think that I would trivialize God with such an insignificant request. Not wanting to trivialize God, I stopped praying for parking places and since I estimate that at any given time there are about three million vehicles in Madrid with only some two million parking slots, this means that at all times there are always a million cars circulating looking for someplace to land. The next time I had to find a parking place in front of their apartment I searched fruitlessly for 20 minutes and then left my car in a vacant dirt lot three blocks away. After that I decided to pray every morning for the parking spaces I'd need throughout the day, but resolved not to mention the subject again to my hosts. I felt guilty about not acknowledging God's gracious choreography of such a small item, but I knew my Spanish hosts were not open to changing their views—and I needed parking.

I do pray about everything. If it's in my day, why not pray about it? It upsets some people when I tell them I always make it a matter of prayer when I've lost something. My children all know that it is useless to come ask me to help them find something if they haven't already prayed asking the Lord to show them where it is first. In my view this is part of the Lord's choreography. It's disturbing when I lose something, so why not ask for divine assistance? I'll admit there have been a few items that never showed up, but for the most part I feel that God helps me keep collected and organized. And I appreciate that help.

It makes no sense to me that some are uncomfortable with a prayer-answering God. "According to your faith be it unto you" (Mt 5:29). It's scriptural. "You have not because you ask not" (Jm 4:2). But the Bible also emphasizes how God likes to be appreciated. "Abram believed the Lord, and he credited it to him as righteousness" (Gn 15:6). It would seem that many find it difficult to *believe* the Lord but God likes to be believed! I'm convinced that's why God's presence is everywhere to be seen. Just as freeways here in Los Angeles would indicate God's mercy on the micro level, so you only have to contemplate the heavens to see how God's grace operates for us on the macro level. It's been over a year since the Shoemaker-Levy-9 comet fragments plowed into Jupiter—a planet 300 times the size of Earth. The other day one of our neighbors, a Jet Propulsion Laboratory scientist, casually mentioned that after a year the holes in Jupiter's crust made by these fragments are still larger than our entire earth. It doesn't take much imagination to figure out that there, but for the grace of God, goes our planet home.

I'm convinced that the same God who keeps thousands of people from crashing into one another on the highways and byways of life is obviously protecting our Earth from loose cannons shot off from passing comets. As the Psalmist tells us, "God has set the moon and the stars in their places" (8:3). We displease the Lord when we do not acknowledge God's protection and verbalize our trust in the Lord. The Psalmist bewails the fact that "both we and our ancestors have ... done wickedly" because "we did not consider your wonderful works nor remember the abundance of your steadfast love" (106:6-7).

The Lord's choreography in every moment and aspect of our lives is apparent for any who stop and consider. Moment by moment we live under God's mercy. Instead of sniveling and murmuring about our circumstances and our difficulties, we should rather pray and ask that if it be God's will, this cup be removed from us. If it is not, then we must stand with Christ and not put God to the test by flinging ourselves down from our own personal parapet expecting angels to intervene. Rather we should center our thoughts on the Lord, praying positively, remembering that the earnest prayer of a righteous person "availeth much" (Jm 5:16). As Jesus taught his disciples: "Whatever you ask for in prayer, believe that you have received it, and it will be yours" (Mk 11:24).

I believe this divine T.L.C. (my version renders this as Tender Loving Choreography) is done to entice us into hurling ourselves on God's mercy constantly, asking for our daily bread, praying that our guardian angels keep us from harm and danger, evil and accident. I've decided that's why savings accounts don't work for me. No matter how often I try to sneak an extra day's provision by, something happens to upset the plan. God wants me on a short leash. It's daily bread I'm promised, not a guaranteed annual income.

So much in the American society tries to buffer us from what we even call "acts of God": insurance plans for every conceivable problem of health, wealth and the pursuit of happiness; social security and pension plans to blunt aging; defense and security systems to preclude our being vulnerable to attack; subsidies for the rich; disability and welfare systems to palliate our greed and keep us from providing alms for the maimed, the halt and the poor who will always be with us. And then we try to call ourselves a nation "under" a God we are supposedly trusting.

The tension in learning to trust in God's providence is between fatalism—throwing up your hands and saying "Allah wills it"—and boldly approaching God's throne and demanding divine intervention. This is where my morning devotions help, for I lay my day before God and say, "Please guide and protect me, showing me the path I am to take this day." And then I stop, look and listen.

Repeatedly Jesus said, "You who have ears, listen." That used to seem so obvious, almost redundant, until I figured out that it meant learning to read your circumstances; hearing the still, small voice; following the distant and faint signal. I have found that especially when suffering and sorrow come your way, you need to stop. Pay attention. Take heed. Quit flailing about, whining and complaining. If you have committed your life to God's keeping, there's got to be a reason this moment has come your way. Be attentive to the Spirit's moving in this circumstance.

There are a lot of mysteries around God's choreography, but the overarching enigma is the problem of pain. Certainly more brilliant theologians than I have grappled with this subject, but still everyone must ultimately acknowledge that our flawed life brings us all face-to-face with anguish and distress along our pilgrimage journey. Life is a fatal disease no matter how you insulate or bolster it. Our tendency is to ask what a good and loving God could possibly have in mind by allowing such misery to exist. If God is all-powerful, why has God allowed sorrow to enter our world? Worse yet, why did our loving Heavenly Father send his beloved Son to earth specifically to suffer a grievous death at the hands of those who were willing to torture and gall him? And all the while, as we know, Satan continues on his walka-bout, seeking whom he may devour, pretty much free of any external suffering, as far as one can see. Kindly explain.

Well, I can't. But I do know that if you accept these two underlying premises: 1. God loves you much more than you can imagine or think and 2. God is in every moment of your life, then the logical conclu-sion you derive is that no matter what happens, you can be assured that your loving God has a purpose in this occurrence. It is not a Christian preoccupation to worry about bad things happening to good people, because the entire Christian paradigm generates from the cross. God, who declared vocally and supernaturally at Jesus' bap-tism and again at the transfiguration with almost the same words reported in Matthew, Mark and Luke: "This is my Son, whom I love; with him I am well pleased," also refused to let "this cup" of suffering be averted from the beloved Son.

It's a mystery, but as we traverse this vale of suffering we cannot rail at a God who does not love or care for us. Rather we should ask God to show us what lesson we are to learn from this pain, what message we are to take from this hardship and what, if any, new direction we are to follow. As Kierkegaard points out, "It is in the inner life that suffering teaches, and God hears us our lesson, and obedience is the test that is exacted" (*Gospel of Sufferings*, p. 56).

I do everything possible to circumvent pain, avoid hardship, screen out difficulties. Yet the letter to the Hebrews tells us that even Jesus "learned obedience from what he suffered" (5:7). Why should our sinless savior have to learn obedience? And in such a harsh manner? Kierkegaard said "the school of sufferings fits us for eternity," but the creator of the universe already possessed eternity. So for what kind of obedience did Christ suffer?

I know not the answer to that, but I do know that a fourth principle of prayer is important: *Since God is in every moment of our lives, we should never despair or give up hope.* There is always some reason for whatever we are going through. We need to stop, listen and then pray that God will intervene on our behalf in this moment, in this need, in this difficulty.

PRAYER FOR GOD'S GUIDANCE

Loving God, we acknowledge that our lives are in your hands. We commit this day to your watchkeeping and dedicate ourselves to you and your service. Guide and protect us throughout this day. Orchestrate our comings and goings and help us be responsive to your direction. Keep us from presumption and give us appreciative hearts. We ask that in your multitude of mercies you will receive the prayers of your people who call upon you and grant that we might know and understand what things we ought to do. Grant us the grace and power to accomplish faithfully the tasks you give us to do; through Jesus Christ our Lord. Amen.

5.

God's Preëminence

"Worship the Lord your God, and serve Him only."

(Mt 4:10)

Christ's third temptation is the most subtle. Few of us can sing "I surrender all" with any authenticity. Mostly we bow down and worship power, prestige, property or position. And then wonder why God seems so remote from our lives. Prayer helps keep life in perspective, but we are all so corrupted by our ambience that we need constant vigilance to try to understand what Christ's third temptation means for us.

For this round the devil had taken Jesus up on a very high mountain and showed him all the kingdoms on earth and their power. Then the devil promised him, "I will give all this to you, if you will bow down and worship me" (Mt. 4:9).

How many times do we hear people justify less-than-honorable behavior because it's all for a noble purpose? They are going to do an extraordinarily commendable project and the end will surely justify the means. Much of the time we don't even bother to justify our "good deeds" because we are so confident that like the Pharisee in the temple, God is pleased with our religiosity.

The other day I bought a Bible designed for young people for one of my Brazilian granddaughters who is learning English. I thought it would not only be helpful for her studies but it would also give her an incentive to read God's Word. As I was contemplating what brilliant moralism I should write on the "presentation page" I flipped over to the acknowledgements—the first page of text in this book. I paused, saddened by the first line. Tragically, the compilers—all, I'm sure dedicated, God-fearing scholars—of this document lauded in the first words of this version the fact that this had been the "best-selling edition of the Bible in the United States" shortly after it was launched. This was the preëminent factor about this project which they noted. Not that it had been a tremendous blessing, not that it had been a means of making thousands take God's word seriously, not that it had sparked new interest in young people to serve the Lord—but that it had sold well.

This team, who certainly considered themselves dedicated—and successful—followers of Christ, felt that the greatest recommendation for this version of the Bible was not that God had showered grace, mercy and love on all who had participated in bringing out this text, nor that they anticipated one day to hear, "Well done, good and faithful servant" (Mt 25:21 or 23), but rather that it had turned a profit for those who published it—proving its material worth to our materialist society. We are so immured in our culture by the mentality carefully passed down from generation to generation of temple money-changers that no one involved in this best-selling edition of God's word took exception or pointed out how incompatible such a statement would be vis-à-vis Jesus' admonition, contained therein, that "Ye cannot serve God and mammon" or, as this version puts it, "You cannot serve both God and Money" (Mt 6:24).

Not that we don't need money in our society, but we are colossally blind to how much we worship money instead of God. Every time I try to buy something on sale, I know that I am venerating the dollar. Fending off the crowds in order to get more "stuff" for my money means that I don't trust the Lord to give me my daily bread or to supply all my needs "according to his riches in glory by Christ Jesus" (Ph 4:19). Or perhaps I suspect tomorrow God is going to be miserly with me and not give me as good a life as I want, so I make sure that I put my energy into getting the best "deal" possible, even if this means groveling in dirty warehouses, being served by insolent and ungracious clerks—who are obviously suspicious of my motives and assume that I and everyone else in the establishment are out to pilfer anything we can get our hands on. So I submit to demeaning security measures, unpleasant surroundings and intolerable lines all because I think I am getting a "bargain." The lilies of the field have taught me nothing—but the lure of acquiring material things has gripped me firmly.

I began to get a glimpse of how strongly money rivets our attention after spending a few weeks in Colombia and Ecuador with indigenous peoples who basically live outside the cash economy, with nary a suspicion that bargain basements exist or warehouse sales entice or inventory closeouts beckon. Since they do not have a money-based culture, they are not enslaved to materialism as we are. Locks, security systems, health care plans, insurance policies, old-age pensions, fences and garage sales simply do not mean anything to these people. They've certainly got their own problems, but our form of materialism is not where their challenge lies.

How oblivious we are to these matters has fascinated me ever since I returned to the States. After having lived in that remote corner of Brazil for 15 years, I found my friends often would ask me if things had changed a lot during my absence. I tended to say, "Not really all that much—except for acrylic grapes (which seemed to show up in all my friend's homes) and garage sales (a societal innovation that appeared equally ubiquitous)."

What amazed me was how people now were trying to turn their junk and leftover "stuff" into cash. And strangely disquieting to realize that the needy, the lame and the blind were no longer the recipients of our discards. Rather we expected the Great Society to care for them while we went about our business of accumulating the accoutrements of the good life, trying to turn our trash into cash—forgetting the biblical injunction against harvesting to the edges of the field and leaving the gleanings of our life-style to the poor, the halt and the stranger (with or without a green card). Everyone, inside and outside the church, was doing it. Rummage sales seemed to be the fund-raiser of choice for every Ladies' Aid society in the country. Materialism had seeped into every crevice of our community and we were inattentive to any Scriptural mandate that unmasked our miserly ways.

In those days I was writing articles for various religious magazines including some rather radical evangelical journals. For them I could write pieces that questioned the propriety of the military draft, our system of taxation or the exploitative marketing of dangerous products to the Third World poor, but there were no takers when I suggested to the editors an article on "The Sin of Garage Sales." One editor disclosed that he eked out his meager salary through such—and he believed firmly they were an appropriate way to live a frugal life. Having lived for years on what came out of missionary barrels, I decided it would be biting the hand that had fed me and my family to pursue the subject, but I was convinced there was something deeply flawed about how we as Christians handled our leftovers. Even as a "Christian" society we could not take seriously the implications of what Jesus was talking about when he said, "Woe to you who are rich, for you have already received your comfort," or "Give to everyone who asks you, and if anyone takes what belongs to you, do not demand it back" (Lk 6:24, 30).

With my days in the jungle in Brazil now behind me, one of the joys of "civilization" was being back among people who challenged me and nurtured me in the faith. Edith Drury was one of these. A remarkable older woman, she was now dying after having spent her entire life in arduous mission work. A real trooper, Edith could regale us with splendid stories of her frontier mission work. As I got to know her better, it did transpire that she was from a Boston Brahmin family reared among

94

people of great privilege and even was a life member of the Cranberry Club, called by some the country's most exclusive women's association because there is no need to apply, you have to be born into this clique. Yet even though she came from wealth, Edith imbibed the frugal standards of her New England ancestors from birth. Nothing pleased her more than saving money and caretaking her "stuff."

After retiring from mission work Edith devoted herself to caring for Agnes Sanford, a parson's widow who was an aging saint and who had been a forerunner of the healing ministries that have become manifest in various Christian churches in the latter half of this century. A few years after Agnes' death, Edith succumbed to a malady that enfeebled her and slowly brought on her own death. In order to come home from the hospital Edith arranged for round-the-clock care, which she could easily afford. During this period I tried to visit her as often as possible and on her good days would bundle her plus her wheelchair into the car and take her out for lunch or some fresh air.

Over lunch one day Edith asked if we could stop on the way home and pick up some of her favorite thin chocolate mints. She grumbled because she knew her nurses were stealing them and she was powerless to prevent this. I countered with, "Well, you know what the Bible says: 'If someone steals from you, you're not supposed to ask for it back'— in fact, you're supposed to give them more.'"

Edith, the daughter of a distinguished minister of the Gospel, reared in a world dedicated to Christian-based education, a woman who had been teaching the Bible for years and from whose Bible studies I myself had derived great blessing, was indignant. "It certainly does not," she protested.

"It does too," I countered. "I'll show you when we get home!"

After settling her back into her rented hospital bed and carefully caching her new box of mints where she could watch them, I leafed through Edith's Bible to let her read Luke 6:30 for herself. She shook her head with a grim look but made no comment. (It's difficult to take instruction from someone you consider to be your protégée.)

I kissed her good-bye and headed back home thinking about the myriad times Edith must have heard and read that verse without ever having the eyes to see or the ears to hear what Jesus was saying about how we should treat our property. How assiduously everyone in our culture ignores that awesome verse, "So therefore, none of you can become my disciple if you do not give up all your possessions" (Lk 14:33).

Church history shows that those who are not equally blind to our worship of materialism are people we find threatening. The "old, old story" we love to tell in our churches is not about giving up our material blessings and following the Lord, bereft and penniless, as St. Francis did. Rather we tend to concentrate on putting on new roofs, paying the heating bill, fund-raisers to make that possible, and gathering in new members who in turn can share the burden of putting on new roofs, paying the heating bill and the staff salaries—and in the process make us look like a growing, illustrious and successful church.

The other day I went to a baptism in a Catholic church in our neighborhood. The first time I saw its tall, open Romanesque tower built of interlocking arches I exclaimed over the shells that decorated each vault. If this church had been in Spain those shells would have been taken as an announcement that any pilgrims wending their pious path along the *Camino de Santiago* were welcome here. Traditionally these holy wayfarers carried such shells on their belts to use as drinking cups and to announce their pilgrimage intentions to all they passed, so for over a thousand years hostels who welcomed the pilgrims and churches which were stations along the way carved some form of these shells into their walls as signs to herald their accommodation of the travelers.

I'd long wondered what connection our California church had to the *Camino*, but had never taken the time to step inside. I expected it to be a nice replica of some European sanctuary, but I wasn't prepared for the lavish panoply of multicolored marble on walls, floors and the pillars holding up an ornately carved ceiling. Chapels and courtyards and colonnades extended the sublime ambience in all directions. After the service in chatting with the young priest I asked how it came to be that such an exquisite building was erected in our town. He was most candid when he related that in the early 1920s a priest assigned to this parish felt that the local Catholics were being outdone by the major Protestant denominations in this area which appeared to be in the midst of a competition to see who could construct the grandest edifice for their house of worship. In order not to look like the poor relations down the street, this priest spent the major part of his tenure at this parish in building a replica of a Romanesque church in Italy. So apparently the shells were not a sign welcoming the pious wanderer to worship within, but rather an announcement that this church was interested in keeping up with the Joneses.

I left the church marveling at how ingenuous the young priest was. Such an attitude was seen as so normative to all Christendom that he had not found it necessary to dissemble the true motives of how the edifice came into being. It was not "we felt such a project would announce to the world how devoted we are to our savior;" or "such surroundings would be a sign to all who worship here how our Lord deserves nothing but the best;" or "in this atmosphere we can teach our children true spiritual values." He was totally frank—it wasn't the preëminence of God in their lives that mattered, it was their prestige-level in downtown Pasadena that made this congregation dig deeply to build such a luxurious structure.

The primal instinct of this parish, like so many other churches in our midst, is not to teach its adherents the importance of loving the Lord their God with all their hearts, soul and mind, not to learn to cast all your burdens on the Lord who answers prayers, protects us from evil and delivers us from temptation, but rather how the church can advance the congregant's position in the neighborhood. Join this impressive church and become a winner. A prominent leader in town. An outstanding, upstanding citizen of the community. And in the process become a significant, contributing member of the parish.

I once belonged to a large, popular church whose much-loved pastor admitted not-too-privately that to become a notable member of the congregation you had to pledge a minimum of $2,500 per year to the budget. My first thought on learning this was how poorly those hapless fishermen from Galilee would have done in our midst. No "silver and gold have I none" ministry accepted here! Soon after this, I found myself drifting away. The hypocrisy of this stance was so antithetical to my understanding of the Gospel that I found it hard to enter into the life of the church. Finally I moved to a smaller, less renowned congregation where I could continue to worship the Lord in as much truth as I could muster with my frail faith. And contemplate what role the church has in the spread of the God's kingdom.

Several years ago I published a book, *The Church Without Walls*, which tells the story of a small Protestant English-speaking congregation in Madrid, Spain. They had come together as a missionary church during the years when Franco was trying to carry on the spirit of the Inquisition and make it difficult for anyone other than adherents of Roman Catholicism to survive in that country. For a birth to be registered with the civil authorities, a child had to be given a Catholic saint's name. For anyone to hold public office, serve in the military, or teach in a school they had to pledge fealty to the Roman Catholic church. It was illegal to be a Protestant, build a Protestant church, even sing a Protestant hymn (they'd get you under an ordinance on noise pollution).

Finally in 1967 because of complaints from the growing tourist community (the constant pressures of materialism holding sway), statutes were amended and a limited law of religious liberty was passed. In those days upwards of 20 million foreigners visited Spain annually. Today with a population of 40 million, Spain hosts 40 million tourists a year, so the tourist dollar has been a great boon to their economy and complaints from this sector are taken seriously. Basically this modification of the laws meant that even though Protestants were still illegal, they were tolerated—especially in the large cities.

Still, this small Protestant band of foreigners knew their presence would seem intrusive to many who consider Spain to be an exclusively Catholic country. Rather than put all their energy into building an in-your-face sanctuary (which could not be registered under a church's name anyway, but would have to appear as private property donated for this occasional purpose with no steeple, no bell and no signs allowed), this congregation decided to borrow space — first an unused meeting room from a hotel that catered to the international set, and then after the Second Vatican Council had blown winds of change and ecumenism throughout the Catholic church, a school chapel from some teaching nuns across the street from this hotel.

The years of adversity had forced this congregation to take seriously Christ's command to "seek ye first the kingdom of God and his righteousness," and because of this, the Lord's promise was fulfilled: "and all these things shall be added unto you" (Mt 6:33). Since this parish's energy was not riveted on maintenance, upkeep and improvements, they could concentrate on what it meant to be church — visiting widows, feeding the hungry, caring for the poor, praying together that they might be made into the image of Jesus Christ and thus become a paradigm of the living Gospel.

The "things" added included free, first-class accommodations provided in the beginning by the hotel and then by the neighborly nuns. In a gentle way this band of believers bridged waters that had been troubled by generations of dissension and condemnation. If the medium is the message, then by caring for the needy and the shut-ins regardless of their religious background, this congregation proclaimed far and wide the validity of the Gospel of Jesus Christ while becoming a vibrant community of caring, committed followers of their Lord — a testimony to the living presence of Jesus Christ in their midst.

Most people in the hierarchy of the church are uninterested in how successful such a "Church Without Walls" is because the more walls in your care, the bigger your empire appears to your neighbor, the more prestigious you seem to your colleagues, the more funding base is available for your projects. That is why St. Francis was so castigated by the authorities of the church. Even of his own order. He refused to provide roofs, pension plans or health insurance for his followers. The Franciscans tend not to dwell on the fact that their founder was kicked out of the order in the last year of his life simply because he kept insisting God had told him not to own property. *The Wisdom of the Poor One of Assisi* is a lovely little book written by a French Franciscan scholar which dramatizes the story of St. Francis after returning from a pilgrimage to the Holy Land. He comes back to discover that his order now boasts 4,000 members. To house them properly, the new leaders have acquired several pieces of suitable property.

When Francis remonstrates with them, pointing out that owning anything was inimical to their founding principles which he was convinced were inspired by God, the new superiors point out to Francis how rigid and preposterous his stance is in the face of their current situation. Francis refuses to be reasoned into moderating his standards to meet the present needs, so the new leadership suggest that perhaps the time has come for Francis to move on.

Off he plods to a nearby mountain hermitage, despondent, discouraged and heartsick. After a winter in solitude with only his beloved Brother Leo by his side, Francis emerges from his cave into the springtime and announces that he realizes now that it is enough that God is God. Not that he is successful, or respected, or revered. Not that his order is faithful to the three original postulates, or flourishing or thriving. What matters is that God is God. God is in charge. Finis. Nothing else counts. Shortly thereafter Francis sickens and dies, a man at peace with his maker and his own soul.

It is as hard for us, immersed in our materialism, to leave our property to God's protection as it was for the early Franciscans. But it has been ever so. The story of David's census, told in 2 Samuel 24 and repeated in 1 Chronicles 21, long perplexed me. Whatever did God's curious injunction against numbering the population mean? It seemed so nonsensical. What could be wrong about making a census of the inhabitants of your land? For disobeying, David was given three calamitous choices for a punishment: three years of famine (some ancient manuscripts say seven), three months of fleeing before his enemies or three days of suffering from a plague. Deciding to throw himself on God's mercy, David opted for the three-day plague—which proceeded to wipe out 70,000 people.

God was obviously serious, but what purpose was served by this command? Such heavy-handed judgment would seem inexplicable unless numbering was perceived as a direct link to something heinous. Then it struck me: the possible exegesis is so uncomfortable, we'd prefer not to put it into our lexicon of Biblical admonitions. In the early days of David's kingdom, just as is true today, numbering was a precursor to taxation and conscription. You can't tax people without something like our social security numbering system, nor can you draft them without somehow finding and giving registration numbers to those eligible to be turned into warriors.

So the explanation, taking this command in its scriptural context to its logical conclusion, is that God's children were to be a people apart, who trusted solely in the Lord rather in their own wealth or their own might. There was no need to tax one another and there was no need to draft one another. God would provide. God would protect.

Thus God tried to keep the Children of Israel from falling into the common human pattern of numbering, taxing and drafting. This turned out not to be a specious command, for Scriptures are filled with stories of how God proved to be worthy of the trust that the Lord kept trying to engender: Gideon, with his pared-down army leading a smashing victory over the Midianites; armor-less David with a slight slingshot braving the machinery of the taxed and well-defended Philistines, defeating the giant-shielded Goliath; Jehoshaphat (who was told, "Ye shall not need to fight in this battle: set yourselves, stand ye still, and see the salvation of the Lord with you, O Judah and Jerusalem: fear not, nor be dismayed; tomorrow go out against them: for the Lord will be with you" [2 Chr 20:17]), watching as his amassed enemies proceeded to slaughter each other.

Prosperity and protection were to come from God's hand and trusting in God's provision and might precluded the necessity for filling the state coffers and defense ranks. Even if you are exposed, at risk and vulnerable, you do have the Creator of the universe managing the action. This explains the victory handed to Gideon's tiny band and the wealth and wisdom poured out on Solomon's unworthy head. Conversely, by trusting in their own might instead of God's protective mercy, the Israelites brought down their handmade kingdom and found themselves in Babylonian captivity.

Does this Old Testament pattern extend to us? In the New Testament we find Jesus being consistent with this disregard for the normal protection agencies. "Sell what you have," Christ told the sadly rich. Insurance wasn't big on his agenda. In fact he told his would-be disciples, "If you follow me, you won't even have the security of the foxes with their holes and the birds with their nests." It would be catch-as-catch-can for food and raiment and a place to lay their heads.

As for taxation, to the tricking Pharisees Jesus said, "Render unto Caesar;" to Peter (whom he caught lying about the questionable temple tax) Jesus pointed out the inconsistency of this tribute, then rather than tweak the collective beaks prematurely, he trusted God to supply Peter the coin miraculously from the fish's mouth—though Christ himself did not stoop to get involved with the whole show. This almost-mocking stance which Jesus took toward both Roman and temple taxation, finally provoked the ire of the establishment to the point where he was seen as a dispensable enemy whose very existence was a threat to their social order.

Unfortunately, we are more like the Pharisees who would rather lose their city to the infidels and the Romans than save their souls by living at risk. Not for us this life of throwing ourselves on God's mercies, taking neither purse nor scrip nor shoes as we go about our earthly pilgrimage. Yet repeatedly I have found that God's illogical provision does seem a natural extension if one believes in trusting in the Lord for everything. Every time I have resisted the temptation to hoard, protect and stockpile, I have received untold bounty from God's hands. Living the exuberant, vulnerable life of the foxes and the lilies obliges you to fling yourself on God's mercies. It is a life that takes you to your knees, because only in prayer can you still the throbbing heart, calm the disquieted spirit and rest in the assurance that God is there to defend, provide and surround you with guardian angels.

For years I lived with unlocked doors. As a minister's child growing up in post-World War II America, I lived in a house house normally so full of people that the easiest solution to handle all the traffic was never to lock the door. It made even less sense in Brazil where the doors on our house were so rickety all you had to do was jiggle them a little to make the lock open. Besides, with ten children running in and out, even locking the doors didn't keep them from showing up with total regularity for every meal. Sometimes others chided us for leaving on vacation without locking the house. I'd always respond that it seemed silly to bolt the doors, since everyone around knew how easy it was to spring our latches and get in. So not locking just facilitated the process for anyone who needed to borrow something, and besides, since we were trusting the Lord to guard our gates, we could rest assured that God would protect our property. If anyone stole something, they probably needed it more than we did, for after all the same Lord who had given it to us in the first place, was surrounding it with guardian angels. God could certainly replace whatever was missing as easily as the Lord had given it originally.

When I got back to the States I found this spirit towards property was no longer prevalent. A lot of people in the community vigorously defended their property against all comers with private guards, neighborhood watches and direct hook-ups to local law enforcement offices. At the drop of a bolt, we could have helicopters roaring overhead, lighting up the skies to investigate why a neighbor's security system had been breached. It was impossible to be as cavalier towards property as when I was in the jungles, but still I tried to trust the Lord to protect us.

By this time I was living in a large, two-story wooden house that had survived almost a century of California earthquakes. It creaked and settled and squeaked whenever the wind blew, the temperature changed or a possum crept over the roof. Usually I paid no heed, but on those rare occasions when everyone was gone and I was left alone for the night, the serenity of having the house to myself was shattered whenever those noises started to close in. I would go to bed saying my prayers as usual and trusting the Lord to be my protection. But instead of immediately falling asleep, as is my wont, I'd find myself lying there, eyes wide open, staring into the murky recesses of the bedroom, trying to identify the sources of the various thuds and scrapes and other night noises that kept me awake. After reciting the Jesus Prayer to myself for awhile, I'd get up and lock the bedroom door and finally fall into a less-than-heavy sleep.

In those days we had an obstreperous old cat who would scratch at the side French doors to be let in. When you went to open the doors, she would often stare at you and then continue to languish in the sun, unmoving. Finally, I had her number and got it down to a system—I'd open the door, let her come in when she felt like it, and then close the door once she was inside.

On a couple of mornings after one of these disturbed nights I'd go downstairs to make my first cup of tea only to discover that after the last foray on the French doors the night before, I'd managed to forget to close them after the cat meandered in. So the French doors had stood ajar all night. The first time this happened, I laughed. To think of my huddling under the covers afraid of the night when here I'd left the door wide open so anyone could have walked in unhindered. The second time I finally got the message. Obviously the Lord was pointing out to me how incapable I was of providing my own protection. Instead of worrying about dead-bolting and double-locking the house, I needed to pray and ask God to guard me and then rest in the

Lord. As Hebrews says, "We are his house, if we hold on to our courage and the hope of which we boast" (3:6). Here I was, claiming to be a member of God's house but unable to trust the Lord to watch over me through one simple night's sleep.

This minor lesson has transformed my life. Each time I have been tempted to be afraid, to resist a challenge because of the prospect of risk, or to cringe at what danger an adventure might bring, I remember our absurd open French doors and how God had protected me through my nights of fear. Surely whatever hazard I was about to face was as easy for my guardian angels to handle as watchkeeping me through my nights alone. And so I pray, turning my life and limbs over to God's defense. By holding on to the courage and hope of which I boast I have had wonderful escapades in many corners of the world where I've gone with the assurance that I was surrounded by guardian angels. I'm not foolhardy, but I do trust in the Lord for my protection.

Everything in our world tells us that such illogical Biblical commandments are no longer applicable and that we should provide our own safety nets, draft our own armies and put together our own defense systems. Not wanting to argue the case for a just war, I do believe that God is in charge of all the wars and rumors of war that Jesus promised would persist throughout the ages. Yet how easy it is to take full credit for what has been done for us supernaturally. When I was publishing in Brazil, I brought out in Portuguese a wonderfully inspiring book, *Rees Howells Intercessor*, which tells the story of the director of a little Bible school in Wales who became a great prayer warrior—learning to seek God's face and pray through whatever problem faced him or his school.

During World War II after lamenting the terrible carnage from the London blitz and wringing his hands over the many defeats at the hands of a satanic Hitler, Howells decided that as a body of Christian believers they needed to pray the war to an end. It wasn't going to be through their own might and power that they won this war, but through God's divine intervention. Soon a pattern developed: Howells would seek God's face and ask for discernment and then when he felt the Lord was leading them in a certain direction, he would challenge the entire student body to a period of fasting and prayer until they felt "released" or assured that their prayer vigil was completed.

Howells' journals are replete with intances when his little band of Christians would take on various campaigns and pray them through to victory. Even though censorship and news blackouts caused a time lag in public disclosure, when once the information was released, they discovered the timing was too consistent to be coincidental. It had to be miraculous that when they felt they could stop their regimen of prayer and fasting, what they had been praying for had already happened.

This has been an inspirational book for many, including myself. Whenever I've recoiled from a prayer campaign that seems too formidable, I recall the totally incredible reversals that Rees Howells and his little student body prayed into being: stopping the seemingly invincible Rommel on his race to the Suez Canal which would have secured the Fertile Crescent and the Eastern Mediterranean to German control, even Rommel's inexplicable absence from the front for the D-Day invasion that left his troops scrambling and leaderless for those crucial first days of the Allied landing.

History buffs who pore over the records of that war repeatedly comment on how small incidents—seemingly insignificant turnings—altered the course of that great diabolical confrontation. Yet half a century later as we commemorated battles and truces and the cessation of fighting, I heard no one emulating the Psalmist who praised the Lord for decreeing victories, admitting: "Through you we push back our enemies; through your name we trample our foes" (44:4-5). Even with the Cold War behind us we hear precious few who would follow the Psalmist and say, "I do not trust in my bow, my sword does not bring me victory; but you give us victory over our enemies, you put our adversaries to shame. In God we make our boast all day long, and we will praise your name forever" (vv. 6-8). Rather, we hear Christian politicians, television evangelists and people who claim to be "God-fearing" make jingoist statements striving to increase the military budget and expand our arsenal so we can defend ourselves against all comers.

The truth is that we are seldom willing to leave our future to a God who would send his beloved son to earth to die. All our defense strategies, our insurance policies and our health plans are to shield us against "acts of God" which we deem unbefitting to our station in life. Basically these protective measures are an extrapolation of the acts of rebellion instituted by our progenitors in the Garden of Eden when Satan convinced Adam and Eve that the fruit of the knowledge of good and evil was in their purview. They should be the ones to decide what was best for their lives. Flinging themselves on God's mercy all the days of their life would only mean that they would be denied what was pleasant to look upon. The good life was within their reach. All they had to do was pluck it from the tree that God had put outside their jurisdiction.

The first tenets of a defense plan were instituted in that moment for it was at that point they perceived themselves as vulnerable, naked, in need of covering, clothes, insurance policies and a bomb shelter. But just as surely as God found the cowering Adam and Eve in the Garden, God finds us no matter how buffered and protected we keep ourselves. At the end of the trail we must make an accounting of what we have done with our talents, how we have walked with our Lord, how we have trusted our Maker to protect and provide for us during our earthly sojourn.

Which brings us to a fifth principle of prayer: *God wants to be our provision and our protection because the Lord wants to be preëminent in our lives, not the court of last resort.* We should thus be encouraged routinely to make such things matters of prayer. We probably will never be able to sing, "I surrender all," but we can daily meditate on how far we fall far short of worshiping the Lord our God with all our heart and strength. At our point of weakness we can ask God, out of the Lord's infinite mercy, to give us faith to trust the Lord a bit more each day.

PRAYER FOR GOD'S HELP

Almighty God, the source of protection and security, the fountain of all wisdom, who knows our needs before we ask and our ignorance in asking, have compassion, we beseech you, upon our infirmities and those things which for our unworthiness we dare not, and for our blindness we cannot ask. Mercifully give us protection from our enemies, sustenance for our daily needs and faith for our journey. Keep us mindful of your willingness to listen to our requests, your ability to grant us more than we could ask or think and the safety which is ours when we rest in your strength and succor. We ask this through Jesus Christ our Lord. Amen.

6.

God's Healing

"If you ask anything in my name, I will do it."
(Jn 14:14)

This preposterous promise of Jesus has proven true repeatedly in my life, yet much in our world tells us that such illogical Biblical commandments are no longer applicable. Some remarkable gainsayers to these modern notions have come into my life, impressing upon me that the Gospel message is still totally relevant.

Over the years I have become aware that God has consistently provided me at all stages of my development with at least one if not several "older women" who have interacted with me at a level impossible for my mother, who, for reasons of her own, abandoned me emotionally at birth. These have been spectacular, spiritual women who have prayed for me, nurtured me, cared for me and directed my steps all along my path. Every one of them has taught me priceless lessons about walking with my God. Yet perhaps the most profound lesson I learned from them all was that each of them had feet of clay—each of them had spiritual blind spots which would obviously extrapolate to the fact that I, too, could expect ever to see through a glass, darkly.

I met Edith Drury of the thin mints because of Agnes Sanford with whom I had established a correspondence. Agnes had written seminal books on the healing ministries of the church and in one letter she invited me to call on her should ever I visit California—which I eagerly did during my next visit to the States. When I phoned, Agnes asked me for tea one summer afternoon. Sitting on her shady balcony in the foothills of the San Gabriel mountains, we sipped iced tea and began a friendship that lasted until the day she died. Our wide-ranging conversation skimmed along as brightly as the summer breezes which stirred the lovely oak trees that climbed up the canyon below her house. Several times as we talked on topics related to prayer and healing and how God deals with us rather unworthy servants, Agnes would comment, "I'm so glad Edith isn't here. She would never have let you in and we wouldn't have had this great discussion."

Agnes was particularly taken with the fact that Jimmy, her favorite blue jay, who came hopping along the banister demanding bounty, proceeded to eat birdseed out of my hand as well as hers. A quizzical look entered her sparkly blue eyes as she mused, "He's never gone to anybody else before." Never having been mistaken for St. Francis, I later decided the Lord allowed Jimmy's acceptance of me as a cryptic signal to Agnes who from then on always seemed to welcome my presence.

Before I left that first afternoon Agnes asked if she could pray about anything for me. I admitted I was in turmoil trying to decide what to do with my future. She said, "That's easy enough," and took me down to her little basement office where she preferred to pray. As she laid hands on my head, I felt immense energy flowing through her hands as she lifted my requests to the Lord with whom she had had such wonderful rapport those many years. Just as Jesus had felt the power flow out of him when the woman with the issue of blood had touched the hem of his garment, I felt the power flow into me.

Then it was that almost like a bystander I watched the unexpected and shocking events which began within the next twelve hours. First my mother-in-law died that night and this event pulled the small string that turned out to unravel my life in Brazil. The question I have never been able to answer is why I put up with George's abuse and unfaithfulness for so long. For many years I did what was expected: We had been taught to be thankful for everything, to accept the lot God had given us, to be submissive to the authority placed over us. But each year as I tried to gunnysack my emotions, I got angrier until finally after one horrible episode I exploded and announced I had to get away. It was arranged that I go to Spain for a six-month sabbatical, staying with friends so that I could write while my two youngest attended a "real" school for the first time in their lives. From there we continued to the States to visit relatives, but I could not bring myself to return to Brazil—until after that encounter with Agnes.

The next morning I was awakened with the news that George's mother had died in her sleep in Texas. Within days he was back in the U.S. for the funeral—which gave us a chance to try to talk out our differences. Again I heard the pledges and the promises. He vowed if I would try one more time and return to Brazil, he would pay for my trip back to the States along with Heather and Heidi any time I wanted to leave. I was feeling guilty about abandoning my eight adopted children—even though most of them were now grown and living off the *fazenda*. Still, we had not come to any closure—so once again I believed those hollow words.

Within days he was back to his old patterns and within months (after having taken a glorious three-week camping trip with the entire family where we had time to say good-bye and let me explain why I was leaving Brazil) I was back in California. I was determined to attend seminary and make a life for myself away from the mission, my family and George. Throughout my time in Brazil I had put my efforts into facilitating other people's agenda. I suddenly realized that it was okay for me to get a life as well.

Seminary was heartening. Ever the good student, I found a milieu where I thrived. I loved the academic exchange, the stimulating conversations, the opportunities to interact with other scholars. However, after all my years in Christian boarding schools with their obligatory chapel attendance, I tended to ignore our voluntary chapel services. Then one day an announcement in our weekly bulletin about an upcoming chapel piqued my interest: it was to feature Edith Drury, Agnes's cohort, who would be talking about the healing ministries of the church. Agnes had retired from a public ministry several years before, but Edith still spoke occasionally about the prayer of faith to local church groups.

Back in California I had been hesitant to contact Agnes again, but I was rather curious about this Edith who would not have allowed me into Agnes's sanctum had she been around the previous summer. I decided to attend chapel, but sat in the rear of the sanctuary. At the end of the service Edith invited any who would like prayers for healing to remain after. Having lived virtually disease-free through 15 years of the tropics, I had been shocked to discover days after returning to the U.S. that one of the last things I'd done in Brazil was to contract a virulent form of hepatitis which kept me bedridden for a month. I was still suffering from aftereffects from this bout—plus some apparent parasitical problem that kept my stomach churning and my system out of kilter. The doctors in California had little experience with tropical diseases and seemed annoyed by my untrained guessing.

When I had first called and made a doctor's appointment because I thought I had hepatitis, the doctor acted as if I was a hypochondriac in search of attention. Knowing how infectious the disease was, I was shocked when the receptionist directed me to a chair in the rather crowded waiting room. I tried to find an isolated corner until the skeptical doctor was prepared to see me. He then casually asked me why I thought I might have hepatitis. When I told him it seemed as though the whites of my eyes were getting yellow and my urine was darkening, he realized I knew that of which I spoke. So I wasn't surprised when, after taking a sample and running a preliminary test, he rather anxiously ushered me out his rear door and told me he'd call me. There was no need for me to come back.

The only thing I could do was sleep it off—and try to keep from itching (easy to say, but harder to observe since the malfunctioning liver deposits so much lactic acid in the system it tends to collect in each cell of the body—which in turn sends scratch-out signals that easily supersede any mind-over-matter commands I've been able to develop). As a parting shot the doctor advised me to send everyone who had interfaced with me since returning to the States to their own doctors to get hemoglobin shots—which would help ward off any spread of the infection. His rather frosty response to my jungle-generated problems made me hesitate about looking for further medical help Stateside.

But instead of being off-put by my ailments, Edith appeared genuinely pleased when I told her I wanted prayer for what I was convinced was a tropical parasite. (Later she divulged that in her experience most seminarians ask for prayer only for money to pay their school expenses, so my request came as a welcome change.) When your stomach which has been distressed for weeks suddenly reverts to calm repose and your system tilts back to normal, you know you've been healed. That night during my prayers I thanked God profusely and then asked the Lord to show me what all this meant.

I'd finally figured out that one reason I'd gotten the hepatitis was that the Lord wanted me to stay in California—and the disease was a wonderful anchor. For years my Minnesota relatives had been making noises about how nice it would be for me to return to the land of my birth. This had seemed like a very attractive option, but when I told them about my hepatitis, I suddenly was treated like a pariah. Some even acted as if they were putting themselves at infectious risk talking to me on the phone. An empty apartment belonging to one aunt was no longer as available as it had seemed. Heather and Heidi, now twelve and eleven, were apparently going to be more of a problem than at first blush. "Etc., etc., etc.," to quote the King of Siam.

So it was to California I was bound and I filed the hepatitis into the "Explained" box. Now this new experience with Edith made me wonder. Surely the God who had kept me healthy through all those jungle years and who had answered innumerable prayers for healing for all my children during that time was also in this moment of my intestinal problems. Perhaps what God was saying to me was that this woman, whom my tendency was to suspect because of Agnes' earlier comments, was worthy of my trust. The Lord was obviously blessing her ministry and I was to pay attention. There was something more here.

During the chapel service Edith had focussed much of her message on the "healing of memories," an insight which had come to Agnes early in her ministry of healing. The next morning I called Edith and told her about the miraculous improvement in my stomach problems. Then I suggested that what I might really need was the healing of memories. She agreed to meet with me that week and it was incredible. This one encounter liberated me from so much of the excess baggage I was carrying around with me. There was the burden put on my shoulders by parents who early had abdicated their responsibilities of nurturing me. There was a spouse who put enormous energies into being duplicitous and violent. And there was a missionary community who were unsupportive and judgmental. It was not that my history was blotted out, but rather that a healing unguent was poured over my wounds.

Edith and I had met in my apartment. Before praying, she looked around my seminary digs with its nauseous brown shag rug, the hand-me-down furniture I had assembled from those departing these sacred halls and the limp drapes stained by ranks of scholars who had gone before. "Don't you know God wants you to have joy in your life?" Edith demanded. I hesitated an agreement. She continued in her abrupt way, "How can you have any joy living in this dump?"

The seminary would have been less than pleased to hear her summarily dismiss their housing, but trying to see it through Edith's eyes I realized it probably came across as rather dreary. After the primitive, abstemious home I'd left in the jungles, I had thought it good

114

enough until she pointed it out. To sparkle it up I had filled it with colorful plants and bright prints—and I was rather proud of the shelving I managed to put in myself with the help of a patient clerk at the hardware store who walked me through the steps of how you toggle bolts into wall plaster. Besides providing the bare minimum inside the apartments, to minimize gardening expenses and maximize their earnings off the students, the seminary had concreted most of the patio, so it was less than the best place to bring up my girls. I knew Edith was right.

Having convinced me to raise my sights, Edith proceeded to include in her prayer for the healing of my memories, a request that the Lord would miraculously provide us with proper housing. Why not? That evening I sat down and added to my prayer-request list which I kept in my Bible a detailed record of the requisites I'd need to have joy in a home—a nice house in good repair with green grass and shade trees, half-way between the seminary and the girls' school, a fireplace and a large kitchen. It seemed a bit audacious to ask for, but within six weeks circumstances had evolved that allowed us to rent half of a house that met exactly all those specifications.

Once again, a simple prayer wrought marvels. Not only was the bitterness rooted out of my affronted heart, but this was the beginning of a grand friendship that lasted the rest of Edith's life. Soon we fell into a pattern. On Tuesdays when Edith was in town to lead a weekly prayer group, we would meet for sandwiches at a little pie shop. Then Friday evenings I'd go to Agnes' house for a prayer meeting. As she was now approaching 80, Agnes was spry and healthy but getting forgetful, so sometimes her prayers would trail off in the middle of a sentence as she got slightly muddled. At that point Edith would deftly take over to keep Agnes from humiliation and the prayer meeting on course. Edith was determined to invite a few people who understood the situation to come around for these weekly sessions so Agnes could feel she was still involved in an active ministry.

s here, week after week, that my prayer life was nourished and
hese women trusted God and gave God the glory for all the
that God interceded in their lives. Agnes' formula for the
er of faith was simple but effective: First you quiet your soul
until you have the confidence that what you're wanting to pray for is
in fact something that is in God's will. This was easy if the matter
was scriptural—and that's why it is important to spend time regu-
larly meditating on scripture passages such as Jesus' statement: "I tell
you for certain that if you have faith in me, you will do the same
things that I am doing. You will do even greater things, now that I
am going back to the Father" (Jn 14:12) and "I promise that when
any two of you on earth agree about something you are praying for,
my Father in heaven will do it for you. Whenever two or three of you
come together in my name, I am there with you" (Mt 18:19-20).
Other scriptural promises can embolden us: "Every good and perfect gift comes down from the Father who created all the lights in
the heavens" (Jm 1:18) and "Dear friends, if we feel at ease in the
presence of God, we will have the courage to come near the Lord
who will give us whatever we ask, because we obey and do what
pleases the Lord. God wants us to have faith in his Son Jesus Christ
and to love each other" (1 Jn 3:21-23).

Having the confidence that you can come boldly asking for whatever your desire is, you proceed to the second step which is to describe
whatever you're praying for in faith-language—positively imaging
what is going to happen now that you know God is going to intervene
on your behalf, painting a word picture of the limb healed and active
or portraying the situation free from difficulty and barriers. Then
when you have firmly gotten hold of a positive picture of what is
going to be done by God, stop and thank the Lord—the third step—
for the work already done and promised because Jesus said, "I am
going back to the Father."

Using these three simple steps, I have seen wonderful things happen in my life and the lives of those I love. And, contrary to what

many Christian leaders have tried to explain to me, I have found that the God of the universe—who sang creation into being and who puts the myriad stars in their courses—doesn't prioritize a willingness to do what we ask according to how noble our cause is.

The other day I was telling a prominent member of our church—who sees himself as a pillar without whom the nurture and organization of our congregation would barely proceed—that my future son-in-law had a wonderful answer to prayer about a sewer line on the house he was building. After he asked God to intervene on his behalf, an inspector had come back to remeasure a disputed distance. They found a three-inch variance from an earlier calculation that saved him literally thousands of dollars. My church friend disdainfully asked me if I really thought that God cared about sewers.

Why not? Doesn't God care about those inconsequential sparrows? God probably even counted all the fleas and no-see-ums and tarantulas I killed while I lived in Brazil. (To be truthful, I never actually killed the tarantulas, but Zezão, my oldest son, always said you could tell the size of the spider by the decibels of my screams and he'd always come to the rescue and slay those dragons for me.) Even though I wanted such exterminated from my life, I knew that in God's sight they were as worthy of note as the number of hairs on my head. I would never bother to get a hair count. Christ obviously used this illustration to point out how God is involved with the minutiae of our lives. Even the fleas and spiders were part of God's creation and I owed them healthy respect. However, I must say, had I been on the planning committee, they would never have come off the drawing board.

After my jungle sojourn, I had my bite-protection system down to an art form. Once when I was visiting the Motilones in northern Colombia, I was sitting in the shade on a grassy knoll in front of the clinic at Iquiacaroa on a warm afternoon talking with Bruce Olson who has been a missionary with these tribal peoples for over 30 years. Genetically Bruce is half-Norwegian, half-Swede and from Minneapolis so we have a lot in common. It was the time of day in the tropics when I knew the no-see-ums started on their main course. In Brazil I made every effort to go indoors and stay behind screens during this risk period, but when I suggested to Bruce we move our venue to a less exposed spot, he launched into a rhapsody about how he allows his body to become immune to the effects of such bugs by letting them bite him and then making sure not to scratch, because that's what irritates the skin. It might be uncomfortable, but a little bit of discipline is all that is needed and within a few weeks your autoimmune system kicks in and you aren't even bothered by such.

In some ways we were playing who-has-endured-the-most-in-the-jungle with each other, but it wasn't a fair field—you could hardly compare cooking, cleaning and raising a large family in a primitive setting with taking on arrow wounds in a native long house. However it did seem a bit wimpy not to follow suit so I watched his exposed ankles (he had on only sandals, I at least had socks covering mine) fill with those tell-tale pinpoints the no-see-ums leave behind. For the next month as I scratched and clawed my body raw—in a most undisciplined manner, I grant you—trying to eliminate the poison from my system, I decided that Bruce's being a half-breed must have made the difference. I, after all, had four Norwegian grandparents and genetically was not formed to endure tropical pests. Bruce's Swedish southern exposure made it work for him, but that painful month convinced me that never again would I willingly leave myself vulnerable to such attack.

I do not know why God created fleas and no-see-ums and mosquitos. Nor why viruses and germs and diseases are in the breezes. Even though we all know the inevitability of what our future holds, we spend an enormous amount of energy denying death. Fleeing from it. Putting it off until the last, raspy moment, we pursue healing and remedies and convalescence with all our might. It is part of our primal instinct for survival. Even Christ prayed that the cup be passed from him. But the beloved son shared with all humanity the one certainty of our being—an ever-approaching death.

Death is a subject we tend to find infinitely uncomfortable. In our society we sanitize and cosmeticize it to keep from having to reflect on the subject. Even though for a believer death should be considered "a happy ending" for any life story—because to be absent from the body is to be present with the Lord—still we act as if the silent reaper is our worst enemy. Scriptures tell us that death entered the world through sin, but the Bible also assures us that through Christ we have conquered death.

Moses summed up the whole of the Pentateuch for the Israelites; "I have set before you today life and prosperity, death and adversity. If you obey the commandments of the Lord your God . . . you shall live. . . . But if your heart turns away . . . you shall perish" (Dt 30:15-18). Apparently not even the desire for immortality kept the Israelites on track, any more than it keeps us there. Just as I fell an undisciplined victim to the no-see-ums poison, so we all succumb to the choices that eventuate in our death. Like the Israelites, we turn deaf ears to God's decrees. Earlier Moses had explained to the children of Israel, "If you listen carefully to the voice of the Lord your God and do what is right in his eyes, if you pay attention to his commands and keep all his decrees, I will not bring on you any of the diseases I brought on the Egyptians, for I am the Lord, who heals you" (Ex 15:26). Miriam's leprosy and Moses' death before entering the Promised Land showed that not even they could take this good advice. All around us is evidence of the connection between sin and disease and death.

Jesus also linked sin and disease when he said to the paralytic, "Son, your sins are forgiven." Much to the disgust of the Pharisees, the lame man "got up, took his mat and walked out in full view of them all" (Mk 2:5, 12). Granted, it wasn't a sure-fire formula. Later, when his disciples asked the next logical question: whether the blindness of the man who was blind from birth was due to the sins of his parents or to his own, Jesus gave them an illogical answer: "Neither this man nor his parents sinned, . . . but this happened so that the work of God might be displayed in his life" and then proceeded to restore his sight.

Again, this healing infuriated the Pharisees, who hauled the ex-blind-beggar before their tribunal to demand, "How can a sinner do such miraculous signs?" urging him to "Give glory to God," because "We know this man [Jesus] is a sinner." Then came the ex-mendicant's wonderful response: "Whether he is a sinner or not, I don't know. One thing I do know. I was blind but now I see!" (Jn 9:2-34).

Healing is an area which seems to threaten church authorities. It's not neat. It can't be regulated or ordered. You can't write procedural guidelines, canons or rules that control healing. Too often healing happens around the mavericks, the marginalized, the uninformed, the undisciplined. Our bodies and how they operate are mysteries to everyone—trained physicians and illiterate peasants alike—so why the healing ministry of the Christian community is seen as a spiritual danger to so many is perplexing to me. Why not ask the God who knit us into being in the first place to restore to health and strength whatever has gone amiss?

A few years ago I was in Rome at a mission conference and there had an opportunity to meet Archbishop Milingo from Zambia. Apparently he had been raised to the archbishopric before the powers in Rome figured out he had a gift of healing. Ours was an academic group of missiologists—missiology being the science of mission and the field in which I got my master's degree. At our periodic gatherings around the world, participants are given the option to extend their visit by a few more days to have an "exposure" experience to what the church is doing in that locale. That year we voted to go to Rome because an opportunity had come about to include a visit to the Secret Vatican Library—which isn't really secretive, but is off-limits to all but the select elect. It contains rare and wonderful documents to thrill any academician's soul. (We saw the pope's copy of the excommunication of Henry VIII plus Henry's much-sealed and signed official appeal—denied—plus the Diet of Worms—for the Protestants in our group—and various ancient papal bulls. The librarian couldn't put his finger on the bull that drew the line of demarcation giving

Brazil to Portugal and the rest of Latin America to Spain; I'd asked to
see that one. Regardless, it was a great treat.)

For my "exposure" experience I had chosen "the healing ministries
of the church" because of my interest in this area and my friendship
with Agnes plus all my experiences in Brazil. The interview with Archbishop Milingo was just one of many "exposures" organized by our
leader Christoffer—a young, precise but gracious campus minister
from Heidelberg. We were carted around to hospices and hospitals—
including St. John of God's on the *Isola Tiberina*. For 400 years this
Catholic order has cared for the sick on the site of an earlier Temple of
Aesculapius where 2,000 years before that the quarantined sought succor on this boat-shaped island in the middle of Rome's Tiber River
making it, our guide—a "Do-gooder" brother, as the Italians call the
John of God monks—assured us, the longest, continual spot of healing ministry in the world.

Archbishop Milingo is ensconced in an apartment just kitty-cor-
ner from the Vatican gate where the medieval-garbed Swiss guards
disdainfully examined our passports and papers giving us access to
the library. There were nine of us from all over the world that chose
the topic of healing ministries, and Christoffer was quite pleased he
had managed an appointment for us with the archbishop—a rather
elusive figure just then in Rome. Our group was looking forward to
meeting this man who had become almost an outcast in the view of
the Catholic church because of his healing powers. We happily
trundled ourselves to his apartment at two o'clock the last afternoon of our "exposure" only to discover that due to the siesta hour,
the apartment's doorkeeper was asleep, the gate was fast shut and
there was no way to find him to importune him. Our resourceful
German leader stood examining the bank of apartment intercoms
and finally pounced on one of the buttons. (I was impressed by his
deducing that such a well-known person would put up a few obsta-
cles to keep the curious at bay—like having the only no-name but-
ton.)

A woman's voice asked us what we wanted and Christoffer answered in plausible Italian that we were here to see Archbishop Milingo. Christoffer had guessed right, because she informed us sweetly that this was indeed the archbishop's apartment. The bad news was that he was gone to Perugia and wouldn't be returning for a fortnight.

All of us who understood a little Italian looked at each other somewhat nonplussed. Finally Justin, a black Jesuit from South Africa who had done a doctorate at the Gregorian and thus was the most fluent Italian speaker of our lot, stepped to the tiny mike and in a rather clipped English accent explained to the voice that we were a group of academicians with an appointment set up weeks before with the archbishop for that very afternoon.

Later I asked Justin whatever possessed him to try English and he shrugged. Obviously she was speaking Italian with an English accent and he wanted to make sure she understood we were not just another group of Italian curiosity-seekers. In English, the woman remembered that the archbishop, indeed, did have an appointment with a group of missiologists, but unfortunately he had been tied up in Perugia and they didn't expect him back for another hour (at least this was a bit better than two weeks).

Afterwards we decided she'd been in Rome too long to tell us the whole truth all at once. One of our group, a woman from Indonesia, had done her doctorate in Switzerland. Unfortunately, in the process she hadn't been imbued overmuch with the mind of Christ, but she had acquired the Swiss' fanaticism for promptness and was utterly irate that the archbishop was making us wait. When we returned in an hour the English nun finally let us inside the apartment. We had to step over a mother and her teenaged son who had appeared in the interim and were sitting on the apartment stoops waiting patiently for a glimpse of the archbishop. We assured them he had not yet arrived. We were being received by an assistant. They begged us to help them see Milingo.

Sitting in the archbishop's sparsely furnished front room we tried to make small talk with the English nun who was rather nervous because our Indonesian friend had come in harrumphing about how inconvenient it was for Milingo to keep nine people waiting with no notice aforethought. Finally the nun suggested brightly that we might want to see a documentary made by the BBC on the archbishop's situation. That took up another hour, but still no archbishop.

It was, however, informative. We learned that in 1973 Milingo received the gift of healing. From that date forward wonderful healings occurred when he laid hands on the sick and prayed for them. During most of the Eucharists he celebrated, people in the congregation were spontaneously healed. In Africa (much of which makes Brazil look like a developed nation) word of this phenomenon spread like wildfire. Literally thousands trekked across the savannas and the steppes and the deserts to attend the Eucharists he celebrated. In the midst of this mushrooming popularity came the word that the pope wanted to see Milingo the following day.

With no farewell, no closure, no parting words, the archbishop scurried off on the next plane to obey his church leader, only to find himself languishing for the next 18 months while the pope turned out to be too busy after all to see him. Finally Milingo's humble obedience to this virtual house arrest got him a hearing with the pope, who eventually told him, no, he could not return to Zambia (rumors are that a neighboring prelate with a lot of pull resented Milingo's enormous popularity and engineered this withdrawal) but, yes, he could celebrate the Eucharist once a month, not in a church proper but in the basement of a hotel on the outskirts of Rome.

Milingo wasn't being defrocked, just reassigned. His new role was to be in charge of the Vatican's Immigration and Tourism—which is little more than a figurehead position, but it was hoped he would thus be kept out of mischief. Healing being a transportable gift, within a short while of being allowed to have this slightly public ministry Milingo was back in the news. The documentary brought his story up-to-date showing that again thousands—now mostly Italians like the couple out front—were flocking to his monthly Eucharists concelebrated with 27 priests from all over the world. And again remarkable healings were occurring at every service.

The most pathetic line in the BBC documentary came from the Czech cardinal who headed up the year-long inquiry into Milingo's African ministry (out of the same, ancient office which handled the Inquisition!). Staring straight into the camera he pontificated to his interviewer, "As you know, healing is not central to the gospel message." We gasped and wondered what gospel the curia had that placed healing at the margins of the church's life.

The documentary over, we were told word had come from Perugia that Milingo was finally on his way, but it would be a couple hours still before he'd arrive. We went back to our lodgings for our evening meal and finally the call came. The archbishop would receive us at nine p.m. The Indonesian again grumped, but accompanied us back across town.

Having just seen the video, it seemed as though we already knew this simple, humble spiritual man who came in and apologized for not being able to get back earlier. A benefactress was wanting to donate property to create a healing center in Perugia and it had taken longer than he had expected. His eyes twinkled as he said he hoped that we didn't mind doing things on "African time." Then Milingo launched into a discourse on healing and handed out a signed paper that he had given to a curial institute on "The Healing Mission of the Church" (maybe instigated by the cardinal's ludicrous statement to the BBC). At the end of an hour's session he looked at the nine of us seated in a half-circle, and offered to pray for each of us. He told us to tell the Lord silently what it was we requested, then he went around the circle and prayed for each one, laying hands on our heads. At that moment there were no more sophisticated academicians in our group, for we all could sense God's presence and came as humble mendicants. Even our Indonesian friend was uncharacteristically awed into silence and bowed her head along with the rest of us.

It was a hushed group that made its way back across the paving stones that stretch out in front of St. Peter's. There were no words to explain. As with Agnes, from Milingo's hands too I felt there emanated a palpable energy. A friend in the group had suffered a chronic cough for two years which immediately improved and then disappeared within six weeks. My own request was a bit more esoteric, but nevertheless I knew that as of that moment it was taken care of—and it was.

Milingo and I don't share identical views of theology or ecclesiology, but I know the God who has blessed him with this extraordinary gift is the God who heard my childish plea for healing from measles. I was confident then and am convinced still that this God was and remains willing, against all odds, predictions and expectations, to step in miraculously and bring healing. I am aware this does not always happen. I have an older sibling who was deafened, in part because of my mother's negligence. In order to go off to an evening meeting with my minister father she left the baby with an inexperienced teenager who unfortunately let the baby get chilled. This brought on a high fever that burned the nerve endings in the ear. I don't understand why this took place. I know my mother has never been totally sane since that dreadful event and I don't know why healing for this harrowing disability was never granted to her many requests.

Ever after this my poor, tortured parents, in spite of being good, staid Lutherans, exposed us to one healing ministry after another as they sought remedy for my sibling. A lot of good has come from this trauma—including a deaf school founded in Brazil where literally hundreds of deaf children who had been tucked away in darkened corners of farm shacks were given a chance to come together and learn and communicate and get a life. But healing remains a mystery.

It is inexplicable that for all the years I was raising my ten children at the end of the jungle trail, we virtually never had to go to the doctor. We did go to the dentist a lot, and I still am grateful to Dr. Alfredo who took care of all our children's teeth while they were growing up. Every time I'd go into his office determined that it had gone on long enough and demand he give me a bill for his services, he'd always claim to be too busy to do it right then, but he would get to it forthwith. He never did, and ever since I've asked the Lord to reward Dr. Alfredo generously for all his many kindnesses to our family.

Nor am I claiming that the children were never sick, but I early developed a habit of asking their guardian angels to protect them from harm and danger, sickness and accident. And when they fell ill, I always prayed for divine intervention. Never will I forget the night seven-year-old Cota got sick. In one hand I was leafing through the *Home Medical Book* checking out the index, while with the other I was trying to comfort her as she threw up blood and bile and mucus. She looked horrible, and it didn't take long to figure out that her feverish, yellow-and-blue face, plus her hacking chest meant she had pneumonia.

I had one of the children go call our Brazilian minister who lived next door asking him to come because we needed prayers for healing right away. As we prayed I held Cota's hand with one hand and placed my other hand on her forehead. Before we had finished praying, her forehead was no longer clammy hot. That was strange. I opened my eyes and saw that during our relatively short prayers, her complexion had returned to being pink. The rasping noise was gone from her chest and her breathing was normal. Still I got out the medicine chest, put her in a cot next to my bed so I could watch her through the night and told her she didn't have to go to school the next day because I simply couldn't believe that what I'd seen with my own eyes was a miraculous cure.

By noon it was impossible to keep this bouncing child in bed, so I apologized to the Lord for my doubts and told Cota she could get up. As C.S. Lewis explained in *Miracles:* seeing is believing only if you have a category for belief. Without one, miracles simply are not perceivable. Even though I believed miracles happened, my first tendency was to doubt. However, with every passing year in Brazil my category for believing in miracles grew as I watched the Lord intervene in matters large and small, momentous and not.

Cota is now closer to 40 than she is to 30 and has children who are taller than I am. A few months ago we talked about this incident and I asked her what she recalled of the healing. It had seemed to me that ever after that evening, Cota had been a different child and that there had been a healing of her spirit as well as a physical healing. She seemed not to be as cantankerous and selfish as she had been, though she was never the saint Vera was from birth. I always assumed her pneumonia had been a means of getting us to pray seriously for her healing—in body, mind and spirit.

That evening is imprinted on Cota's memory as deeply as my measles scene is on mine. What most impressed her was that from that night forward she was freed from terrible nightmares that had tormented her. Her birth mother, who had led less than an exemplary life, was a spiritist and had surrounded Cota with all the hocus-pocus of occultism. I had not known any of this, but inadvertently, as it were, we stumbled on the relief package.

All those years in Brazil, in fact, it felt as if I was involved in an incredible coöperative effort with the Lord. Definitely I was the ignorant, unskilled junior partner. Of course I was too inexperienced to handle the job given me, but there was no one else, so God was stuck with me. The Lord seemed willing enough to step in and there was no doubt in my mind that God was my "refuge and strength, a very present help in trouble." I loved that passage from Psalm 46: "Therefore we will not fear, though the earth give way and the mountains fall into the heart of the sea." As I learned to "be still and know" that God was in charge, I saw miracle after miracle happen. Probably if I'd been more mature, if I'd been given adequate resources, if I'd had more support, I would have missed out on these wonderful experiences. But it was just I and the Lord with this immense ordeal.

I know God didn't answer my prayers because I was so deserving, or had such tremendous motives. The Lord knew well (because I complained often) that I had stumbled into this situation much against my will and my better judgment. But I had not turned back. I have a compulsive nature—I have to finish what I start. This is not always good, but it did keep me in Brazil until I felt I'd gotten my discharge papers from God (maybe the Lord was tired of my kvetching and said, "So, go, already!").

Strangely enough, all the blessings promised to those who care for widows and orphans and those in distress have continued to pour out on my head. Even so, if I had it to do all over again and had a choice, of course I wouldn't. But I don't, so I did. And I'm glad I did, because I know we are all better for having shared with one another this life together. But in my view it wasn't a choice anyone should have had to make. But then neither was the cross, so we're back where we started. God does the choosing. We obey. Or try to obey. Or pray for help to try to obey. Or importune the Lord for help when the difficulties seem overwhelming.

One lesson I learned from Agnes involved the spiritual power that comes from participating in the Eucharist. I first wrote her while I was on that sabbatical in Spain to thank her for her forthrightness in her autobiography. After years of living with the phoniness and duplicity so rife throughout the church world, what I found charming in this book was Agnes' candid telling of her story. I could relate to this woman who had trials and tribulations as well as successes and victories. And that's what gave me the impetus to write her—and in turn receive an invitation to come visit should ever I be in California. I wanted to tell her how inspiring her story was and how I was finding solace and healing in the Eucharist services I was attending, bringing to the altar my troubles and compulsions and watching the Lord ease these out of my life—miraculously.

I don't know why all this intercession for healing works, only that it does for me. It certainly gets one's attention. Peter claimed that God used such phenomena as a certification process for Jesus who was "accredited by God to you by miracles, wonders and signs, which God did among you through him, as you yourselves know" (Ac 2:22). Thus Peter explained to the "utterly amazed" curious folk who came to see what all the ruckus was about on the day of Pentecost when the violent wind and the tongues of fire and the speaking in various languages by this group of unlearned fishermen would indicate to the most cursory observer that something was up.

Obviously these were some of the "greater things than these" Jesus had apprised them would happen because he was going to the Father. So Pentecost was the beginning of their own accreditation process and from that day on, thousands were added to the church because of the healings and the visible signs of God's presence done in Jerusalem and abroad. God got their attention through these miracles just as God gets our attention today. Healing is thus an evangelistic tool — even though in order to perceive miracles you must have a category for belief. I've even known of people who have been healed who continued to refuse to believe in God. Others take an "aw-shucks" attitude toward their healing and more than a few persons have forgotten foxhole promises of what they would do if they escaped that incoming mortar.

We can never fully understand why sickness comes into our lives — whether to demonstrate God's power, to get our attention or because of sin — either ours or someone else's. Neither are there rules to explain when or why or how healing happens. God obviously impresses on us through healing how absolutely present the Lord is in every moment of our life, our suffering, our joy and our sorrow. Which brings us to a sixth principle of prayer: *Ask, and you will receive. Search, and you will find. Knock, and the door will be opened for you.* Until the final healing occurs when all tears shall be wiped away and all sorrows cease, we can rest assured that the Lord who formed us in God's own image is ready to nurture, guide and heal us simply because God loves us more than we can ask or think.

PRAYER FOR GOD'S HEALING

Creator God, our times are in your hands. You have promised that whatever we ask of you in the name of our savior Jesus Christ, you will do, so we come asking that you restore us and those we bring to you to health and strength. We thank you that we can rest in the promises that you are always willing to hear our pleas for deliverance. We pray that you might grant us boldness and courage to believe and trust in your mercy and grace all the days of our lives. Make us mindful of our duties to those who need thy healing touch in body, mind and spirit. We ask this through Christ our Lord. Amen.

7

God's Compassion

Lord, you are good to us and your love never fails.

(Ps 106:1)

It took me a long time to comprehend that God's compassion was not tied to my actions, rather the provenance of God's compassion is the goodness of the Lord. God is compassionate to us not because we deserve it but because God is love.

Yet, in turn, our religious world shows so little compassion. For all the love God sows, it appears what the Lord manages to reap in the circle I grew up in is judgment, and harsh judgment at that. My aunt was 90 when she told me she'd never forgiven her sister for getting pregnant and having to get married, embarrassing everyone and besmirching the family name—almost 70 years before. I had always thought of them as the closest of friends—they did everything together—but compassion eluded them all the days of their lives. Her sister had already died, and she could have easily taken that information with her to the grave because I doubt anyone else from my generation knew this, but right up to the end my beloved, sweet, Christian aunt found it necessary to justify her judgments.

No wonder I find it so easy to be harsh and judgmental on myself. That's what was epitomized as righteousness to me by everyone I knew. I was raised in a legalistic world and I have a legalistic streak that goes to my core. In the early days when I started my regimen of reading four chapters of the Bible and prayer every morning, I used to think that on those mornings when I was short of time, I had to concentrate on the reading and skip the prayers. It was as if I had to do my pietistic best to win God's attention and favor before the Lord would grant my requests. Then occasionally when I couldn't get my reading done, but I prayed anyway, I'd find out that God was still there, listening, providing, protecting and being generous to me in ways beyond my comprehension. Even though I hadn't held up my part of the bargain! Finally it dawned on me that there was no bargain. Nothing in Scriptures demanded that I had to merit God's ear by doing my homework. All the despised tax collector had to do was be desperate enough to stand in the corner and plead for mercy—and he got it, while the respected theologian went home self-satisfied but unforgiven.

It wasn't God that had put down the minimum Bible reading requirement—I had. God wasn't being benefited by my devotional time—I was. So if I shortchanged myself, that did not mean the Lord was going to ignore me and not provide or protect. Scripture was a light for my footpath. God, with whom there is no shadow of turning, didn't need a lamp for the feet—I did. I had become legalistic about my Bible reading, making an idol out of my daily four chapters—and what God was really interested in was establishing a communication system with me. So if there was only time for one or the other, the better part to choose was prayer. It was during my prayer time that I listened and meditated on God's interactions with my life. This was always the most creative part of my day, for during this quiet period I could sense God's pointing out to me different choices, reminding me of things that needed to be done, giving me new ideas about how to solve a predicament. I had turned my Bible reading—

which was also a wonderful source of inspiration—into being Martha's kitchen duties. Jesus wanted to liberate me from bondage to my set tasks as much as he wanted to free Martha. Not that everyone didn't enjoy the fare that came out of Martha's kitchen, but sitting at Jesus' knee, listening, was the better part. The food could wait. It was a secondary concern.

Perhaps one of the reasons God has answered my prayers so bountifully down through the years was to teach me about compassion—the Lord is much more gracious with me than I am with myself, and certainly than my world ever was. In fact, being good to myself is one of the hardest lessons I've had to learn. This also seems to explain why so many in my circle were irritated to see how God blesses me. When I finally left Brazil—to get a divorce, no less—I asked God for two trips every year. After all those years down on the *fazenda*, I pointed out to the Lord that since I'd been stuck in that remote setting for so many long years could I please travel abroad two times a year.

And that is what has happened. Instead of being punished for breaking the rules, I got adventure.

Some would consider this a pretty frivolous request—but what's wrong with laughter? Even though many of my trips have been work-related, I've enjoyed every one. I've been to Russia and Israel, South Africa and the Philippines, Korea and Ecuador, Australia and Peru, China and Zimbabwe, Kazakhstan and the Fiji Islands, Thailand and Colombia, Tasmania and Hong Kong, most of Europe and Central America, a lot of the Caribbean and of course Brazil, Argentina, Venezuela and Chile. Some of the trips have been free, some have been subsidized, some I'd never go on again, but all, I believe, have been given me by God. Even Edith used to get bothered by all my traveling. When she was alive I'd always ask her to pray for my trips, and she would, but grudgingly. Then I'd come back and report how serendipitously the entire enterprise had been choreographed and how God had blessed all along the way. She would be pleased, but she just could not understand my need to head for the horizon every few months.

I think legalism is so endemic to our system that we are too blind to see how creatively God deals with us. Just because the Lord asks you to do something one time, does not a legal tenet make. It drove the disciples crazy when Jesus would say something outrageous and then just when they'd extrapolated it to an obvious doctrinal statement, he'd say, "No, not at all." Like curing the blind man born sightless so the works of God should be made manifest. I beg your pardon? You now claim this person was blinded by God so his healing would show God at work in their midst? What were they to think? What did Christ mean? Why did he keep changing his story?

Maybe our beloved St. Francis fell into this same trap. God told him to strip himself of his worldly possessions—which he did literally—and then proceeded to beg his wretched way into the courts of the highest potentates of the church and state with astounding success, thousands flocking to follow his lead. During the several years he was missing in Crusader action, his followers acquired the property which resulted in his withdrawing from the group that was called by his name. But perhaps Francis had made an idol of not owning property and it was time to listen afresh.

I know this syndrome is something I've observed in many Christian institutions as well as in my own life. One of the reasons I didn't leave Brazil sooner—aside from the kids still being at home—was that it was so obvious that God had worked supernaturally to bring me to Brazil. I figured my Brazilian sojourn was immovable, set in concrete, never to be altered. So after years of railing and grousing—and asking God why someone didn't put a quick end to George's life span—I finally asked the grown-up question: Can I leave? and got the incredible answer: Why not?

Why not indeed? Let me explain why not. . . . But the conversation was ended. Door closed. You want to leave? Go.

This instruction was so shattering to my preconceived notions of what was acceptable in the Lord's sight that I asked for three definite signs—one being Cota's future. We'd had a problem with her two years before when at 15 she had eloped with a ne'er-do-well whom I'd been trying to get kicked off the *fazenda* for inappropriate behavior. George had adamantly refused, claiming he was one of his best cowboys. Then George and I had one of our three-day escalating uproars at the end of which I declared, "I'll tell you one thing, George. If that child elopes with that cowboy, I'm going to divorce you."

"That's fine. Go ahead," he drawled. Which meant that two years later when I did leave he said rather dolefully, "Well, no one can ever say that I wasn't well warned."

However, when Cota and the cowboy went to the judge to get the necessary signature for a minor to marry—pretty much pro forma at that age out in the jungles—the judge absolutely refused on the basis that this cowboy could never give Cota a modicum of the life she had been used to. The judge chided Cota, telling her that daily he attended couples in his chambers who had every material advantage but who weren't able to make a go of it and were trying to dissolve their marriages (at the time Brazil still had no divorce law which meant there were chaotic legal matters implicated in any kind of matrimonial separation). He would be criminal, the judge announced, to sign any papers that would allow Cota to take up with someone who obviously had so little to offer a bride.

We were called by the court to bring her home, but in that jungle culture with its double standards firmly rooted, there were definite entanglements. Even though the cowboy fled the scene, since they had lived together for three days before going to the judge, Cota's reputation was tarnished. Thus two years later one of the three items I asked the Lord for when we were discussing my separation papers was some resolution to Cota's future before I left Brazil.

That evening I was emotionally drained and didn't wait up for the kids as I usually did. Besides Heather and Heidi, there were only four left at home now and they were finishing up high school or going to the local junior college in Xambrê. Since most of the secondary students worked during the day, classes were held at night so the kids would normally get in a bit before midnight. I had just gotten into a heavy sleep when Vera woke me with the terrible news that Cota had not come home from school that night. I leapt out of bed horror-struck. The story came out. The cowboy had been seen in town that day and apparently during their evening recess break he had made contact with Cota and convinced her to elope with him again. She was about to turn 18 when no one had to sign for her. That night I ranted at God saying, "I wanted you to take care of Cota, but I didn't want you to do it this way."

After that horrible answer to my prayer, I wasn't surprised when the next day the two other items I'd asked for were supplied. It was obviously time to go. Later I realized that if I had been able to trust Cota's future to God it might have saved everyone enormous grief, but at the time I couldn't cut the umbilical cord and felt I had to know what her future held. Even after all the years of having experienced that God would supply our every need, would nurture and orchestrate our lives along marvelous pathways, I still couldn't trust the Lord to continue to take care of my children while I was in the States. Our faith is so easily reduced to rubble.

Cota's husband, of course, in the intervening two years had not changed his stripes. Within ten days of their marriage, he had already started beating her and brandishing guns and threatening to kill her—and later the children. After several years of enduring horrendously abusive behavior, Cota was widowed when he was shot in a bar fight leaving her with two small children to raise. When I told Cota the story of my prayer years later and how sorry I was for what she had gone through, she stoically replied, "If remorse could kill, there would have been a lot of dead bodies around."

I could relate to those sentiments, but fortunately the Lord got me out of Brazil before anything more untoward occurred. Within weeks the two youngest and I were back in the States. It was a wonderful end to my years of captivity. I returned to the literary world I loved—becoming the editor of an academic journal and going to seminary. Agnes and Edith came into my life—plus all those trips I was taking.

Then after being single for five years, I decided I needed to find someone to share the rest of my life with. I prayed and put out a very specific list of qualities I wanted in a husband. Brazilian friends laughingly tell me that soon I'll have to put anchors on Albert's trousers because he is so angelic, he'll soon be heading up out of the biosphere. He's not all *that* sweet, but he is a nice guy and someone who naturally is a kind person.

It might even look to some as if God were rewarding me for being divorced. But that couldn't be, so let's not suggest it. What I do know is that my world was furious at my upsetting the system. They didn't want me to justify my actions—nor expect God to be compassionate towards me. To show their disapproval of my sinful behavior, my parents not only refused to come to our wedding, but they also sent reams and reams of sermons about how wrong it was for me to marry a second time (even though my father had performed the wedding ceremony for his older brother to marry his third wife—after *two* divorces, but apparently siblings can have different standards of virtue than offspring).

In the intervening five years my relationship with my family had been strained by what I took as duplicitous treatment. When I was leaving Brazil, I asked my father, still the president of the mission, if I could continue to run the publishing house which I had started and which had been under the aegis of the mission. I wanted to make it an independent operation and offered to give the mission back the $1,500 seed money they had advanced to start me off on this venture. He said that wouldn't be necessary and agreed that by rights it should remain under my management since I was the only one in the mission involved in this project. He signed the document which I drafted and before leaving Brazil I changed the name of the publishing house (so it would have no connections with the mission), created a new logo and explained the system to my distributor.

Unfortunately, after I was in the States, the quarterly report from my distributor was missent to the *fazenda*. Someone decided they could open my mail and they were dismayed to discover I had a balance of over $30,000 credit—which 20 years ago was a considerable fund. At that point the mission committee decided that Papa had made a mistake and couldn't rightfully give me the publishing house (which had been the fruit of seven years of my labor) whereupon I began receiving long sermony letters from him explaining why they had to take the publishing enterprise back. I cried foul and pointed out the injustice of a unilateral decision to break a bilateral agreement, but they wrote the distributor (from another mission) and told them to ignore the signed agreement, a copy of which I had sent them, and from then on the Mission Committee would be in charge of my publishing project—and its credit balance.

They then got my pious German nuns involved. Before leaving Brazil I had published eleven books for them in Portuguese. When the people taking over my publishing venture told them I was planning on getting a divorce, the nuns decided I was too sinful for them to have dealings with—and they took back their books from me, failing to pay for the $17,000 that I had invested in translating their titles into Portuguese. In publishing, translation rights belong to whoever has paid for the rendering, while the original rights belongs to whoever owns the copyright. Technically even though the German nuns held the rights to the works in question, they shouldn't have used my translation without settling with me for what I had put into the project. Since they had a very large and prosperous publishing operation, they didn't need to fleece me out of my earnings. I wrote them citing the story Nathan told David about the rich man with flocks of sheep who slaughtered the poor man's only ewe to feed a traveler who had just arrived (1 Sam 12). But they ignored my protest and wrote back explaining how they could have no further dealings with me because I was divorced and didn't need to pay me for the translation because the Mission Committee had told them to settle with them, not me.

After having worked gratis for the mission for 15 years, I felt terribly betrayed, but I left it in God's hands, who has been most gracious in prospering my subsequent work and providing my needs—and quite a few unnecessary wants besides. I even admit to having a moment of perverse gratification when I subsequently heard that those who had plundered my Brazilian operation quickly ran it into the ground, so it folded after a year.

Having apprised the nuns of the injustice, I had to leave it all in God's accounting books and not worry about it. But a couple years ago I did stop in to see my German nuns one Saturday afternoon. Albert and I were spending a month in Geneva at meetings sponsored by the United Nations and the World Council of Churches trying to get the church community involved in the Earth Summit held in Brazil in 1992. Ever since watching the rain forest burn down around me in the 1960s, I had become increasingly concerned about the environmental problems of the world as I had observed what irreparable damage human greed and cupidity were doing to this gorgeous earth that God created and entrusted to our flawed care and purported protection. On some of my biannual trips I had visited and written about the indigenous tribal peoples, who are especially at risk because usually they have no clue about what is happening to them or to their habitat before it is destroyed and it's too late. In the process they might kill a few oil workers or gold miners, but the ravaging of their lands is inexorable and so I have tried to organize support for those around the world who have their fingers in the dikes, trying to hold back the voracious oceans of industrialized society that will soon engulf these peoples.

The month in Geneva was filled with meetings and interviews and drafting pacts which the nations of the world could agree to in their efforts to save the earth's environment from total destruction. It was fascinating sharing cafeteria tables, riding escalators and walking the halls with diplomats, Nobel Peace Prize winners and those who care about God's green planet. But the Swiss don't like to work on weekends, so during that month we had every weekend free. One we spent hiking in those glorious Alps, wending our way up paths bordered in wild flowers, stopping to take in breathtaking views and think about the beauty of God's creation. Another weekend we rested up and took a much lazier approach to the outdoors, hauling a picnic lunch on a water taxi that stopped along the beaches of Lake Geneva.

The entire time we'd been in Switzerland we'd looked for someone going to Germany who could make a delivery for us. Finally, the last weekend we were to be in Europe we decided to head north ourselves on the autobahn and deliver a portable computer which we were donating to an affable young math professor in Leningrad/St. Petersburg whom we had met when he was doing post-doc work in California. (With two computers, I had been feeling guilty because I knew this brilliant young mathematician—who could do a lot more with one than I could—had none.) He was also trying to cope with the disintegrating Soviet Union—the attempted coup on Gorbachev happened that very weekend. In trying to determine the safest way to get this portable to him we decided it would be best to ask a friend of his working for the summer in a German lab to hand-carry the computer back to Russia.

It was an easy drive on well-maintained roads, even though all along the highway the browning forests glowered down on the drivers whizzing by at close to 200 mph. It appeared no one cared enough about reviving the trees to slow down to ease up on the carbon dioxide emissions that were killing the trees. The directions we'd been given were scientifically precise so we easily found the friend's apartment in the lab's dormitory complex. With sign language, flawed Russian and painstaking English we managed the computer transfer. After a hot glass of Russian tea and a lot of smiling nods, we finally backed out.

The afternoon was still free, so since it wasn't too far from my nun friends I suggested we pop in and visit their chapel. I wanted Albert to see this site which had been such a large part of my start in the publishing world. In the early years I had visited them several times and it was always impressive. They are sweet and gentle and loving and go about serenely in their habits, singing their visitors to sleep each evening and then awakening them the next morn with songs of praise to the God who provides so generously. But they are German—so everything is on schedule and you are graciously invited to follow their regimen—on time. As I recalled, Saturday afternoons were for free time so I hoped we could just make a quick visit and leave.

When I first stayed at their convent, invited to discuss our joint publishing venture in Brazil, I had been living in the jungles for a decade. Although Brazil is not known for being the safest place on earth, even as civilization got ever closer we still maintained our modus operandi that precluded locking doors. Though in a country as corrupt as Brazil, as roads were built and people moved closer the temptation came to be like everyone else and bolt and padlock everything in sight. Still it didn't seem right to me after all the years of asking God to guard our gates to begin acting as if the Lord was no longer capable of being our security. I also did not want to put a lot of energy into securing our empire, thereby giving our household the notion we were controlled by fear. I was confident that the God who had been faithful in providing and protecting our home would continue to do so—and if someone should steal from us, then I would trust God to handle the retribution. I rationalized that whoever might take something from us would not be able to enjoy it because God would turn their ill-gotten gain to dust. If someone wanted to steal from us it was their problem, not ours, and we just asked our guardian angels to protect us from harm and danger and evil-doers.

Besides, I knew there were no secrets where we lived—the jungle telegraph worked impeccably. We were still far enough back off the main highway so every stranger coming down the road was noticed. No one could get away with anything overlooked. In fact, the only times we locked the doors were during storms because it did help to keep the gale-force winds from hurling them open. Basically this system worked. I had a pony stolen once, but everyone knew who stole it and where it was. Scripture said not to ask for it back, so we let it go. We did tell the local policeman—who was as corrupt as the rest of the police force in the country—but since we didn't offer to pay him off, he didn't do anything about it. I never did figure out what God had in mind with that affair, but after praying for justice for a long time I was finally able to forgive the thief and leave it in the Lord's hands.

I was surprised the first time I visited my pious German friends whom I considered to be light-years ahead of me in holiness. (They did, too. They complained affably about my too-short skirts and my pant suits for which they firmly provided dowdy-skirt substitutes to be worn in their presence so as not to contaminate their turf. However a stout wife of an Anglican bishop from India was perfectly free to wear her sari which always exposed her plump midriff, which to my mind was a bit more risqué than my knees.) What I marveled at was how much energy these virtuous nuns, silently gliding along from one locked door to the other, put into keeping their swag of keys from jangling so as not to disturb the tranquility of their manicured grounds. Everywhere you went there were kempt paths, sedate gardens and quiet nooks for prayer—protected by locks, electric gates, closed-circuit TV systems (in the days when these were rare and quite expensive) and security measures. I wanted to ask the nuns why they didn't fling themselves on God's mercy, but felt like—Who was I to suggest to these devout women how they were to walk with their God?

Yet I think I perceived something they couldn't see—and that they wouldn't hear from me because they considered themselves in their nun's habits, with their unsullied smiles and their chaste life-style to be my spiritual superiors. I admit they spent more hours on their knees each day and led a life of devotion inconceivable for a mother of ten. Still I had discovered, somewhere in the midst of cooking and baking and sewing and cleaning, a wonderful truth about God's protection and provision which I would have been willing to share with them. If they could have been willing to dialogue—and listen—I might have saved them some grief. They were clinging to and protecting their property in a manner which smacked of avarice.

They called it good stewardship, but I wasn't surprised years later to meet one of their neighbors—on a beach in Mexico, of all places—who said the nuns had a reputation of going after widows in their area, trying to get them to bequeath their property to their very worthy project. Having had my parting experience with them, I wasn't totally surprised even though I knew they justified their actions because they saw themselves as exemplary Christians. When some relatives of these widows had remonstrated, the nuns insisted on their property rights.

The other area which had always given me pause was their insistence on praying for every morsel they ate. We had similar histories in learning to trust God to put food on the table—they after the war when there were major shortages in Germany, and I in the early days of feeding my family on a pittance. But I had moved on from the sustenance phase. In the process I'd learned some intense lessons about God's providence, but I also knew God had something else in mind when I was put through all those months of deprivation. Surely the God that supplied nature with bountiful abundance was not interested in my living a penurious life ever after. Those exercises had given me a chance to learn to ask for specific requests so I could grasp the overview—God, out of a deep compassion, loves to do good things for us. I also concluded that the food was merely a wake-up call. The Lord wanted my attention so that I would know that God loves to answer our prayers. Food was like kindergarten. After I had the food procedure down pat, we could go on to other spheres where there were new spiritual lessons to be learned.

Thus when these German nuns first told me unctuously that for the past 25 years they had not eaten anything they hadn't raised themselves or "prayed" through the gate as specific items, I wanted to point out that there were a lot more important things to pray about than the bread on their table. Of course God wouldn't let them starve and would answer their prayers for bread, but it seemed obvious to me that theirs could be a much more vibrant ministry if they didn't have to put so much energy into concentrating on food. The God who was willing to feed them was also willing to expand their horizons and take them on incredible prayer-adventures. If they didn't trust their God to feed them (or protect their gates) how could they graduate to the next level? The possibilities were limitless. God had gotten their attention with food when they were hungry, but now those days were over. Unfortunately, they couldn't perceive that they'd allowed themselves to get stuck in that rut. Praying in enough food had become for them almost an idol—something that made them feel superior to the rest of us who went to the grocery store and chose the foodstuffs we would use that week.

Because of their sanctimonious piety I knew they would never listen to suggestions from someone like me. But my experience is that the Lord never repeats a method for supplying your needs supernaturally. Every time I pray for something, thinking surely it will come from this obvious source, it doesn't happen. I'll get what I've prayed for, but from an unexpected corner. This adds to the wonderful adventure of allowing God to be your provision. By insisting to the Lord that all their food need come in through their front gate or otherwise they would starve, the nuns were imposing their Germanic regulations on God. Since the Lord did care about their eating, they got what they demanded, but their strictures were so needless.

Which brings us back to my thesis that no one, regardless of their position in the church or their appearance of piety, has a corner on sainthood. We all have breaches in our wall of holiness. No one is perfectly Christlike. We all could stand good advice from someone with a different perspective. No one can make it on a record of good behavior. We all come flawed. We all need compassion. Consequently no one person here on earth should be set up as the arbiter of our faith, the singular guide to our pilgrimage. Christians need no gurus, for we have Christ. Every single one of us can continue to learn a little more about the peaceable Kingdom until the day we cross the Great Divide and approach the Pearly Gates.

This also helps explain why God answers our prayers: in giving us what we ask for in prayer, God is trying to model compassionate, merciful behavior, hoping we will go and do likewise. But compassion isn't a virtue in wide currency in the Christian world. Judgment and Pharisaism are more the coin of that realm. No matter how costly this turns out to be.

When I took Albert to wander through the grounds of my German nuns' convent, I thought we could do it anonymously, but it was not to be. In fact one of the nuns who had been the meanest to me years before heard I was visiting and came especially to see me and apologize. We shed tears and closed the book on that sad past, but I noted that their once bucolic ambience had been marred permanently. It appears that in the middle of their property had been a legacy successfully contested by an overlooked heir. The courts upheld the heir's right who had built a high-rise apartment that towers above their once quiet retreat. I did not want to think what all they had done to bring about this wake-up call.

We left a bit saddened by the visit to the praying nuns and drove back to Switzerland and the rest of our days of grappling with the ecological issues facing the world community. I kept wondering what wake-up call God might have for the nations of this earth who ignore the issues of compassion, mercy and justice that seem to consume the Lord's attention (see Mt 25:31-46). Even the miracle workers and the most pious are not immune from hearing, "Depart from me; I never knew you" (Mt 7:23).

Of course, we do not always understand the pain that comes our way. I'll never understand the loss of our citrus grove. When I was still living on the *fazenda*, the Brazilian government sent inspectors around our state because someone had pushed through a law saying any citrus tree found within seven kilometers of one carrying a disease called *cancro* was to be cut, burned and a herbicide poured on its roots so that it wouldn't sprout again. Seven kilometer circles basically eliminated all citrus trees from our state if you claimed you found an infected tree every now and then. Later we heard that the big growers in the state of São Paulo had paid off the politicians to get this law passed so they could maintain a monopoly on the citrus market. But it was such a sad day for me as they cut our 500 healthy, verdant trees. I prayed and asked God to relieve us from this onerous calamity, but nothing happened. My distress only deepened a few months later when we befriended the local Catholic priest and found out that "everyone" knew that for a $50 bribe the inspectors left you alone. I looked at his scraggly citrus trees that still stood and thought of our lovely grove of primo hybrid trees that had been reduced to a gray heap of leafless scrub and brambles that had burned in a conflagration that scarred the sky with flames and smoke one horrible day.

Life is so full of gray areas. I have never bribed anyone, but if I had known that for $50 I could have saved those trees, I doubt that I could make that claim today. The "whys" of life are like the poor—always with us. Mostly I don't understand God's compassion towards the greedy and the bad in this world, even though I know—theologically—that my sins have corrupted me as much as Hitler's corrupted him and as much as the greed of those São Paulo citrus growers corrupted them. But I consider myself to be better than they and find no difficulty in judging them as unworthy of God's charity. Unfortunately—in my view—but fortunately for them, God doesn't see eye-to-eye with me on this one. When I really comprehend, at the gut level, what this implies, I can grasp a little what it means when I mouth the truism that God's compassion depends on the goodness of the Lord, not on my rectitude.

Still, the prosperous evildoers are a hard one for me. Maybe it is because I have spent all my days in the Christian world, but strangely enough, most of the cheats, liars and meanies of my life have been religious people who justified their behavior by judging me as being unworthy of decent treatment. I was always amazed that for many of these people the brutality and unfaithfulness I endured in my marriage to George weren't good enough reasons for me to get a divorce.

Those who wanted to renege on promises to me could do so with impunity because I was a sinful divorcée.

The current debate about giving welfare to children of unwed mothers recently engendered a wry commentary in *The New Yorker* on how we in this country are willing to subsidize divorces (through the mortgage deductions allowed to those who divorce and can then afford a second home). In fact the amount of money lost in tax revenue from such mortgage interest deductions turns out to be roughly the same amount we want to take away from the children of unwed teenage mothers—in order to penalize the mothers for having children. The majority of our legislators appear eager to emulate the crowd picking up rocks, ready to stone, not wanting Christ to stop them with that awful little phrase, "You who are without sin, cast the first stone." The author of this article pointed out that since the divorced homeowners tend to be middle-class voters, their violations of "the canons of Judeo-Christian ethics" which accelerate "the decline of civilization" are allowed, and they remain on the public dole (with their mortgage subsidies) while "millions of poor kids will go without to make sure Mom gets the point." Such "virtuecrats" assume, probably correctly, that few unwed mothers and no hungry children are active participants in elections (10/2/95:9).

To punish these "sin children" is hardly to walk in the steps of Christ. Hebrews tells us that Jesus loved righteousness and hated wickedness (1:9) and yet on the cross this lover of righteousness asked his Father to forgive the wicked who scapegoated an innocent person to assure their ongoing power base. Even to his own persecutors he was willing to show compassion. Christ, the sinless one, with every right to be harsh and judgmental, showed only mercy and clemency. Yet we, who call ourselves Christians, are willing to let the little ones suffer in order to make sure their parents comprehend that we will not tolerate the poor who bear children outside of wedlock.

No wonder God showed much more compassion on me in my divorced state than my missionary world, which ostracized and condemned me for leaving my violent and abusive husband. Still this brings us back to the horns of the dilemma: Why couldn't I have shown Christ-like compassion to such a sinner? Why did I still merit God's mercy when I no longer turned the other cheek, went the second mile, emulated Christ by being meek and lowly in heart? And then you're back to the first postulate: God's compassion is based on the goodness of the Lord, not on my virtue. So perhaps the reason God kept answering my prayers in such a spectacular manner was that the Lord was trying to impress on me that I had not become a non-person when I got a divorce.

Disapproval is a strong societal force, and I found that in my mission community I had become a faceless outcast. I was never again mentioned, referred to or invited to participate. I explained this to Albert soon after we were married, but he thought I was exaggerating until one evening when I was traveling and my parents happened to be in town. He invited them to come for dinner and they suggested he might like to see the missionary slide show of the work in Brazil. He agreed, but when it was all over he was flabbergasted. For two hours they showed him pictures that depicted every project I had ever undertaken, all my children, the publishing venture and everything I had constructed in Brazil without once mentioning my name or showing a photograph of me. I had literally "lost face" with my world who could no longer see me.

And my parents always changed the subject if I ever started talking about all the answers to prayers I had. Instead of making me grovel, the Lord was obviously blessing me and showering my life with joy, but they didn't want to hear about it. Fortunately, God's compassion is such that we never lose face with the Lord. Even when our world censures and condemns us, God is still watching over us. There is nothing we can do that will "separate us from the love of God which is in Christ Jesus our Lord" (Rm 8:9).

When the "covetous" Pharisees "derided" Jesus for eating with sinners, he responded with the alarming story of the rich man and the beggar Lazarus. The rich man discounted Lazarus as a faceless beggar subsisting on the crumbs that fell from his table, but by being penurious to Lazarus, the rich man was treated as nameless by Christ. After the rich man died and was banished to Hades, his plea that mercy be shown his still-living brothers and that the dead-but-rewarded Lazarus be sent back to warn them of what to expect, received the chilling rebuff: "If they do not listen to Moses and the prophets, neither will they be convinced even if someone rises from the dead" (Lk 16:14-31). Ignoring the needs of the beggar at his gate was the only crime the rich man was accused of. He wasn't cited for failing to show up at the temple, or forgetting to tithe, or not keeping the ten commandments. He had not loved his neighbor as himself, and that got him on the wrong side of the unbreachable gulf which separated him from the love of God which we have available to us in Christ Jesus.

When I left Brazil, it was hard for me to understand why my judgmental world was angry because God kept blessing me. We were all followers of Luther. It wasn't works that counted, but rather faith—a gift of God, lest anyone should boast! This had been stressed in their catechism, but somehow no one took it to heart. Later, in the midst of getting my seminary degree in missiology, I was trying to work through some of these things with a counselor. He was finishing his Ph.D. in psychology and I felt that in many ways he was too young to understand my situation. But one day he asked: "Why are you still in the world of mission?" I paused. It was the essential question, but one I'd never thought about. Finally I stuttered that it was the only world I knew. He looked at me quizzically as if to say, "For a bright woman, you just don't get it."

Then while we were discussing some of the things George had done to make it impossible for me to stay in the marriage, the light suddenly went on, "I think he's been trying to get rid of me for years!" My young counselor nodded. But of course! George knew he had me in a box canyon. My world didn't care whether I was the victim of physical abuse, unfaithfulness and venomous treatment. They only cared that I not insist on my rights. To get a divorce is to be excommunicated from the evangelical fellowship. You can be guilty of virtually every other sin and still remain within the fold, but divorce severs the ties. Even though it was obvious that George had been trying in all these blatant ways to get me to leave him behind, he knew he would have sweet revenge should I do so, because I would become an anathema to my community if I were divorced.

I walked out of that psychologist's office that day at peace—and free. I knew that my mission world would never again embrace me, so I might as well move on. I finally had the answer that was obvious to anyone with two inches of perspective—I did not need to stay in a community that would forever exclude me. Besides, I wasn't the perpetrator of my divorce. (At least a divorce is an honest sin—so many religious leaders I knew kept up the façade of being married while enduring estranged and hateful lives because they did not want to bear the consequences of being honest about their lives of alienation.) So I finished my master's degree in missiology—I was too close to the end, besides I have a compulsion to finish what I start—but soon thereafter I stopped editing the journal devoted to mission studies. I knew God would continue to love me and care for me and answer my prayers whether I left or remained in the world of missions.

Coming from a community that had compassion only on those deemed worthy, it was difficult for me to comprehend the breadth of God's mercy. Even though I would pray for things because I was needy, I would then stand back in awe as the Lord heaped blessings on my head. I didn't expect the Lord to be this generous with me, but I did know I was in need—and I had two daughters to support.

At an alumni gathering of one of the Christian high schools I had been sent to, the organizers decided to bring in a psychological counselor because down through the years the harsh—really vicious—treatment meted out to the vulnerable student population by the administration had done such damage to their psyches and self-confidence it was felt a time of collective healing was needed.

Reaping what you sow is another reason I think God kept answering my prayers in such a bountiful manner. I treated mercifully the children thrust on me. Because I have suffered want myself, it is easier for me to give to the unworthies who come begging. I know it perpetuates bad habits, but I've got bad habits, too. Mine—like materialism and selfishness—just happen to be more acceptable to my society. I know it sends the wrong message to give alms to those who will probably spend it to support their dissolute life-style, but who asked me, a sinner in need of compassion, to be the judge over them?

It is hard to learn to be merciful to others not because they are worthy—as had once been my criterion—but because they are needy. It is liberating when you no longer have to worry whether the recipient will misuse a gift or when you are able to empower another by trusting and asking God to help that person make good decisions—if not this time, maybe next. Giving away anything with no strings attached is difficult for us because of our materialism. The proper care of our money and our "stuff" is more important to us than the need of the recipient. A gift with strings attached makes us suspicious and, strangely enough, the more suspicious we are, the more vulnerable we are to being conned.

Over the years because of my languages and experience I have taken on some cross-cultural consulting jobs. Several years ago a large Christian aid agency that specializes in caring for children around the world came to me. They had a grievous problem in El Salvador and wanted to try to figure out why they were getting so much bad press in a country where they thought they were doing a great job. The revolution was in full swing so it was dangerous to travel there, but if I could leave within two days I could hook up there with a California-based camera crew doing a documentary for them. There would be safety in numbers they assured me. As a cover to my real purpose I was to tell their people in El Salvador I was writing an article about their operation for their magazine. Since I had written articles for this group down through the years, this didn't seem implausible.

This is the country where Bishop Romero—whom I had met at a conference in 1979 when he was already considered a marked man—was assassinated while saying mass because he had broadcast a warning that it was sinful for his countrymen to be killing each other over land. Rumor also had it that the four American nuns killed there had been targeted because they knew too much. They had worked among the myriad refugees and heard the stories of the indigenous and peasant families thrown off their land in an effort to deny the revolutionaries their support base. Later the compound of the Jesuits would be murderously attacked because, again, they were trying to brake the skullduggery going on. No, El Salvador was not a nice country. I knew I would need guardian angels on this assignment.

After four days of tramping through dusty refugee camps interviewing peasant women trying to eke out an existence in their tarp-tent cities, visiting technical schools where youngsters were being taught employable skills on foot-treadle sewing machines and watching the agency's people operate in that dangerous land, the camera crew flew back to California and I went to Costa Rica to the agency's regional office to hand in my report: Their director in El Salvador did not add up. If he were my employee I'd check out his books with a fine-tooth comb.

As I had winged my way into that country I had prayed, asking the Lord to show me what the problem was here and to bring success to my investigation. It was like peeling an onion—every time I turned around another layer was exposed. Hints were dropped. The director himself was protesting too much. No one said anything openly, but I was constantly being pointed in the right direction. The bad press in the country was the subtle Latin way of telling this foreign agency what everyone in the country had already figured out. No one was willing to tell them to their face (also a Latin trait), but enough people were upset about these misappropriated donations that not one positive mention of the agency's work had filtered into the media.

The regional director protested. Their El Salvadoran director was an ex-U.N. diplomat who had come to them with highest recommendations. He had sacrificially given up a wonderful career to work with them. I must be wrong. And incidentally this was all confidential. I could not discuss what I had discovered with anyone. I did not remember being sworn to secrecy, but I had no need to wash their dirty linen in public. I never heard from this regional director again. Through my grapevine the story came back: their director in El Salvador had stooped to conquer. He'd been siphoning off over a million dollars annually for over five years. My consulting job had saved the agency enormous face—to say nothing of money—because they were able to get rid of him before it came out in the press. And my reward was that this regional director recommended that I never be hired for any further consulting because I was a trouble maker. If I ever asked anyone in the office what had happened in El Salvador I was to be told that I was wrong about their U.N.-trained altruist who had been so distressed by the ungrounded suspicions I had raised that he had voluntarily resigned.

At the time this agency was collecting $10 per month from sponsors to support children around the world. By the time it reached the children in El Salvador, after all the paperwork, the vigilance, the fees, the wariness, the feedback reports, the administrator's salaries and the travel expense, they ended up getting $3.50 a month. I was there. I asked. There were perfectly justifiable reasons why $6.50 went to various expenses along the conduit, some valid, others a bit hazy—like the top executives flying first class because they thus rubbed shoulders with potential wealthy donors. Nevertheless the reasons for all the control factored into their system were based on not trusting the people at the bottom. This money was carefully administered all the way down the hill—and in the process was likely to be siphoned off by unscrupulous people at the top—as happened in El Salvador. (It's been my experience that you don't have to worry about the people working in the dusty camps and walking the mountain trails. Those you can trust because it is their spirit of compassion that keeps them going in arduous surroundings. Watch out for the ones that want to be indulged and have a seat among the powerful.)

I could only compare the modus operandi of this "Christian" organization with what the secular Dutch government had done for the deaf school our mission had founded in Umuarama. This school was a wonderful boon for the deaf children in our area. The wealthy could send their hearing-impaired children to private boarding schools in the big cities, but before this school existed there had been no remedy for most of the local deaf. I don't know how they heard about it, but one day a couple of Dutch representatives appeared and spent the day visiting the school, generally showing interest in the operation. They spoke English and a little Portuguese, explaining they were observing various philanthropic projects in Brazil. As they took their leave, with no fanfare they pulled out a check for $3,000 and handed it to a couple with our mission, telling them they were sure they could put this to good use for the benefit of the deaf children.

It turned out the Dutch government sent such good Samaritans around the world giving grants to those working at the margins of society. Such gifts were powerful catalysts for empowering the little people who care and put their lives on the line. This was 20 years ago and the American couple have long ago left Umuarama, but when I was there recently I went by the deaf school and it was still going strong. I don't know if the Dutch ever came back, but their trusting boost to this project was such a lesson to me.

Especially in juxtaposition with the debacle of the minutely managed Christian aid program in El Salvador, I couldn't understand why this secular body was able to follow Christian precepts—giving with no strings attached to those in need. Jesus didn't ask the rich man to justify himself with an investigative treatise on how Lazarus had contributed to his own sad state and poverty; he just condemned him for not caring. We in the First World are surrounded by an enormous amount of wealth—which carries with it basic responsibilities. As

Jesus said, "If God has been generous with you, he will expect you to serve him well. But if he has been more than generous, he will expect you to serve him even better" (Lk 12:48).

Paul explained it thus to Timothy, "As for those who in the present age are rich, command them not to be haughty, or to set their hopes on the uncertainty of riches, but rather on God who richly provides us with everything for our enjoyment. They are to do good, to be rich in good works, generous, and ready to share, thus storing up for themselves the treasure of a good foundation for the future, so that they may take hold of the life that really is life" (1 Tm 6:17-19). If Lazarus' rich man had observed these precepts, he would not have had his Hades dialogue with Father Abraham because he would have shared his sumptuous feast with those around him who were less fortunate.

In my travels to so many corners of the world I have met remarkable and caring people who are standing in the gap, trying to keep the little people, the vulnerable and the defenseless from being devastated by new structures that are so overwhelming to the unprepared. Some of these are religious workers, others are working on secular environmental concerns, but all of them are deeply dedicated to being "rich in good works." Which brings us to a seventh principle of prayer: *Since the rain falls on the just and the unjust, we know that all people, no matter where they might find themselves on their pilgrimage journey, have equal access to God and can come asking for compassion and intervention on matters of concern to them.*

Compassion is truly the antidote to judging and Pharisaism—both horrible stumbling blocks to establishing the kingdom here on earth. Too often we gloss over Christ's solemn warning and try to ask naïvely, "Lord, when did we see you hungry or thirsty or a stranger or needing clothes or sick or in prison, and not help you?" To which Christ replies, "I tell you the truth, whatever you did not do for one of the least of these, you did not do for me." (Mt 25:44-45).

PRAYER FOR GOD'S COMPASSION:

O God, you declare your almighty power chiefly in showing mercy and pity. Grant us the fullness of your grace that we, running to obtain your promises, may become partakers of your heavenly treasure. Help us to be compassionate with those around us so that we might reflect your glory through our lives. Make us ever mindful that all good things come from you. Give us the grace to confess that Jesus Christ is Lord and to proclaim the word and works of God by sharing your bountiful goodness with all those we encounter. Through Christ our Lord. Amen.

8.

God's Generosity

Good measure, pressed down and shaken together and running over (Lk 6:38).

When I went to Brazil it demanded a bit of ingenuity to live on $50 a month, then $75, with no electricity and a tenuous water system based on a rope pump which was devised to lift water up the 150 feet from our very deep water table to the surface. When something was wrong with the pump, we either survived on the rainwater we collected in our oil drums under the eaves of the houses or we pulled it all the way up by hand out of those deep wells.

In spite of the hardships, everything kept working. Just when the larder was about to implode, a fortuitous boon would replenish it. The pump would chug back to life as the last of the rain barrel water was exhausted. (I did become an expert at hoarding drinking water, which was put through large clay pot filters. We had several of these, including one in reserve in my bedroom for the drinking source of last resort which saved us from having to boil a lot of water from those barrels.) A three-day tropical storm would pound us into confinement just after I had been to town and stocked up with groceries for the next month. As the children finished with one school, the next higher level would be built within easy commute. Or a donation would come fortuitously so they could all go to Bible camp. At every juncture it seemed God was being enormously generous with us.

In the beginning I tried to be as frugal as possible, but after complaining to the Lord about what an abstemious life I lived, I finally got the message—God's handiworks alone would show the Lord does not believe in scrimping. The gorgeous flowers on every hand, the spectacular sunsets that sparkled most evenings, the marvelous tropical birds that winged their way overhead were concrete evidence that God was into being luxuriant. I finally deduced that when my missionary community were being miserly they weren't being godly. They were being miserly.

God was the originator of good measure, pressed down and running over. Still, stinginess seemed endemic to my world. Finally I began to realize that by trying to hoard and save, I was basically declaring my belief that the Lord was capable of providing this much and no more. To trust God meant stepping out in faith and expecting the Lord to come through with tomorrow's needs just as today's needs had been provided for.

The first lesson in generosity for me was to learn it was even okay to be generous with myself—a bit. Then with every miracle I got more audacious. After trying to be frugal and suffer in silence, I realized it had all been unnecessary. Your God is too small, said J. B. Phillips, and I was ready to try bigger. According to your faith be it unto you, said the Scriptures, so I stopped suffering in silence (never my best quality) and decided I needed to take charge of the situation. In the process I learned that God's generosity is inexhaustible. At every step of the journey I discovered how gracious and lavish my God was with us. But it continued to be difficult for me to learn to be generous with myself and with my family.

We were living in an exotic corner of the world, so why not explore it? I arranged day adventures like a picnic at Guaira's *Sete Quedas* (Seven

Falls) on the Paraguay border, which then happened to be considered one of the world's greatest falls. (Since then, some brilliant Brazilian general under the military dictatorship made the peremptory decision to cover them over so that Brazil could have the world's largest hydro-electric dam in the world—an ecological disaster, but they at least managed to build the world's largest boondoggle. The advantages of a democracy are always apparent when one lives under a military rule that admits no questioning of its authority or absurd decision-making.)

Early I'd bundle the family on the back of our four-wheel Jeep pickup along with a picnic lunch to feed an army and a tarp included to cover everyone should a tropical rainstorm develop. I would stand by the pickup to check everyone in as reasonably clean and wearing the clothes I'd ironed (with our brazier-style iron that I had to keep filling with live coals out of our wood-burning stove). Graciano could drive me to distraction. Socks never came in pairs for that child. Even starting out relatively pristine, at the first stop he'd like as not jump off the back of the truck, trip and land in a mud puddle. I'd yell and point out that he wasn't supposed to get out of the truck until someone was there to help him, but he'd look at me so sweetly with his perplexed brown eyes and tell me he didn't remember, he didn't know how it had happened and besides he was truly sorry. How could I stay angry with such a guileless child?

Then the majestic falls would make it all worthwhile. For the swinging-bridges part (best not look down) we had a buddy system matching up the oldest with the youngest on down until you met in the middle, so you had a companion to hang on to or be responsible for as we dangled high above those roaring falls. These bridges connected the islands that interrupted the seven falls, but to get to the largest, *Garganta de Diabo* (Devil's Throat), you had to hike a good two miles, crossing a half dozen bridges. When the wind was right, the spray would sleek down the boards so I'd urge all the kids to hang on to the railing with all their might. It worked because we never lost one overboard, but every year we'd hear of tourists who had wandered too close to the unmarked edge and tumbled to their death. No liability exposure for the park service in Brazil.

In fact, the worst story connected with those bridges happened the last year before the falls were covered over—and long after I'd left Brazil. Everyone was anxious to see the falls before they were swallowed up by the dammed lake, so the crowds were heavier than usual. The government, however, didn't see any reason to repair what was soon going to disappear beneath the rising waters, so there were boards missing on the bridges and you had to walk gingerly to get across. A bus load of tourists were swarming across one of the longer swinging bridges when suddenly an old, frayed cable snapped under the excessive weight, plunging 38 people to their deaths. During the years I lived nearby the dirt access roads were so horrible that few tourists bounced their way to the falls and, besides, the cables were newer so we always got home safely.

Another adventure the children urged on us was a trip to the Paraná River which fed the *Sete Quedas* Falls. Just below the Devil's Throat this three-miles-wide river narrowed down to a roiling chasm you could throw a baseball across. No sonar system ever worked above the noise so when they were measuring and planning for the dam, no one ever ascertained the depth at the narrows. It didn't take much imagination to know that it plummeted deep into the bowels of the earth, for you could stand high above at the overlook and watch huge logs down below be churned into toothpicks as they were sucked into that whirling gorge.

Still considered one of the world's greatest rivers (even the military couldn't stop the tropical rain from falling on that plain— some 60 inches per year with its subsequent runoff), the Paraná River was only a two-hour drive down the dirt road from the *fazenda*. Standing at the river's edge above the falls you knew it wasn't an ocean because even though you couldn't see the far shore, who ever heard of a rusty, brown sea? Also, the horizon was spotted with islands, most of them verdant and green, though a few were nothing more than sandbars that surfaced or vanished as the river rose and fell.

We would rent a boat large enough to take the entire family out to one of the islands that had a good beach and then spend the day swimming, frolicking and picnicking. The boys would try their hands at fishing but nothing much ever came of it. Sometimes we'd buy fish from lads on the island who tended to live half-in and half-out of the water at river's edge and scrounge a subsistence living from whatever was at hand.

These islands could not be purchased because they were between Paraguay and Brazil. For years ownership had been disputed by the two and a settlement worthy of Solomon had been reached: nobody could own the land; it was all subject to military seizure at any moment. Thus the squatters who came here didn't care about such niceties as land titles. But there was also no reason to build decent houses because if they were all that desirable it would just tempt the military into confiscating them. So the island population hung their hammocks in dirt-floored, mud-and-wattle shacks made mostly from the bamboo that grew so profusely here. The years of heavy rains when they were flooded out, they scarcely complained—their shacks didn't take much to rebuild and these things happen, so why be upset? Sometimes the islanders would plant fields, but since so often they were washed away, mostly they lived on bananas and fish and papaya and manioc and whatever came naturally out of the river or the ground. Altogether they were a rather malnourished and bleak crowd.

At least twice during my sojourn in Brazil it seemed as if the only plausible explanation for what occurred involved angels visiting us unawares. Once was at one of those river beaches. We'd grounded our boat on a wide, sandy strand bleached bright by the sun and deposited by the receding, murky river. That year a terrific rainy season had flooded most of the islands, but now the sun was out, the river, albeit thickly rust-brown with the soil runoff from hundreds of miles upstream, was dropping back to its normal level and we were ready to play.

None of the children were yet good swimmers—they were all still young, the oldest being twelve. Since they had rarely been in water over their heads, they had developed minimal water-survival skills. Occasionally we'd go to the local swimming hole in the much smaller Xambrê River that ran along the edge of the *fazenda* to cool off on those afternoons when it was too hot to think, but that river had only a few waist-deep pools where the kids could paddle about. Mostly we took inner tubes and played around or made human flotillas to skim along the pretty shallow stream.

But that day on the Paraná River, the water around our chosen beach was very shallow because of the receding river. Really, it was just an extension of the sandbar we were on and it went on forever with scarcely any drop-off. I had warned the children to stay out of the deep water, but even to get to waist-high water they had to go quite a ways out from the shore. They were gamboling about, splashing and dunking, enjoying the cool when all of a sudden a scream let out. I looked up from where I was watching the smaller ones in water that scarcely came to my calves. Cida and Zezão, the two oldest, were thrashing wildly and shrieking for help, and being pulled under in what obviously was a deep channel of the river.

Apparently they had been playing tag in waist-high water, but with the murk they couldn't see six inches beneath the surface and thus didn't notice the sharp ledge which the swift, deep current had cut in the river. One of them had fallen off that ridge and in the confusion pulled the other one in as well. Now as I raced toward them I saw them flailing and yelling and gasping for breath.

The two were a good 30 yards away when I began sprinting towards them with all my might, but the knee-deep water was too shallow for swimming and too high for easy running. The water dragged at each step. I was besides myself and was convinced they were goners for they surely had bobbed up and down more than the proverbial three times it takes to drown. The gap between us was not closing perceptibly.

Suddenly when I was about to despair of being able to rescue them, out of the corner of my eye I noticed two young lads virtually skimming across the water. They looked to be island squatters, one was probably 15 or 16, the other a few years younger. Both had that lean, lanky look of inadequate nourishment that produces rickety, wiry limbs. But they moved like they were on home territory. Perhaps they knew of a shoal that allowed them to run in ankle-deep water. In any case, they reached the two in time to pull them out, spluttering and spewing water. But safe.

I arrived in time to gather them in my arms to comfort them as they coughed and cried and tried to recover their composure. Then I turned around, seemingly seconds later, to thank our rescuers but they were nowhere to be seen. Gone! Only there was no place to go. At least 50 yards of shallow water stretched behind us with another 30 yards of empty beach before the tree line started. We looked at each other, amazed. What happened to those two lads? No one had noticed. We stared at the open beach that gave us visibility in all directions. Could it be? No! Impossible! But what? They were just right here. . . .

Packing it in for the day, we headed back to the beach and our picnic lunch. A pretty solemn group traveled home that afternoon. I was resolute in my determination that the children were all going to learn to swim immediately. I felt horrendously guilty that I had allowed them be exposed to such risk, but strangely comforted to realize that apparently I wasn't doing this as alone as it seemed. All those guardian angels I prayed for daily were supervising and intervening whenever things got out of hand. But why skinny angels? You would think they'd at least appear as paragons of good health. More like the cherubs of Christmas art.

It was beyond me. What I did know was that in spite of my being inexperienced and inept it seemed I warranted occasional divine intervention. My believing must have been counted to me for righteousness. Besides, I was doing what God wants us to do: take care of the marginalized, the poor, the homeless, the bereft, the orphans and the widows in distress. This isn't an option. The cup of water counts in the final ledger of life. Granted, it was foolhardy for me to undertake this project, but there was no one else willing to step in the gap.

The second lesson I learned about godly generosity is that the more you do for others, the more the Lord does for you. Even if it means guardian angels have to be sent in to save you in a clutch. Since studies meant so much to me, it was vital in my opinion that my children should keep going to school. When I first got the kids, the older ones were attending the primary school on the *fazenda* whose teacher was paid by the state government, but when they graduated from this one-room schoolhouse, there was nothing available nearby where they could continue their studies. Since they all stairstepped in age, these school issues kept accumulating.

Our Brazilian neighbors, who tended to feel that learning the basics was all you needed to survive, were flabbergasted that we were so concerned about educating "other people's children." We tried to explain that they were really ours, but the neighbors would look at our rainbow-hued brood which ranged from bronzed Latin to dark African and check out my blond Nordic features with arched eyebrows. Adopting across color lines was not expected behavior, obviously.

Cida and Zezão being the oldest were the guinea pigs. We tried different solutions including a Christian boarding school which wasn't all that satisfactory because it meant they spent most of their time away. Suddenly we learned that a secondary school had opened near some missionary friends who lived a two-hour drive away over those dreadful dirt roads and who were willing to board them during the week. These two transferred and we worked out a pretty satisfactory system: someone would drive the pair the nine kilometers/six miles to the closest bus stop (half-hour) where they would catch the last bus going west on Sunday evening (hour and a half) and then they'd reverse that route on Friday afternoons after school let out to spend the weekend at home. Of course there were always storms and break-downs and bad roads, but normally the connections were made with no hitches.

One Sunday I found myself alone with the children. Our Jeep driver failed to get back from his weekend excursion and George was traveling. At the last minute I remembered that the driving stint fell to my watch. I rushed Cida and Zezão into the Jeep jitney because if we missed the bus I'd have to drive them the whole two-hour route—and then back again.

I was careening around the curves headed off the *fazenda* before I realized I'd forgotten to get another child to accompany me—which meant I would be driving home alone. In those days in Brazil, a woman simply was never out by herself. She was always accompanied, no exceptions. (The only ones to flout this convention were women of moral turpitude.) It was already dusk and soon that tropical night would close in. I didn't want to think about walking down those dark jungle roads, no flashlight, alone, vulnerable should anything happen to this miserable vehicle. Hastily I prayed asking my guardian angels to keep me from breakdowns, accidents and stoppages along the way and kept going.

I have never understood the current fascination with Jeeps and Land Rovers. Having given up, gladly, the one we had with its isinglass windows you could roll right down to trade for a sturdy, closed-in Volkswagen that kept out the billowing dust and the sleeting rain— and would even float, rumor had it, should we bounce into water—I could never fathom why people that didn't need to, chose to drive such uncomfortable beasts.

The Jeep was making funny noises, so when we got to the bus stop I didn't wait to make sure the kids got on. There were others standing there expecting the same bus, and we had friends nearby for a fall-back position should the bus not show, so I gave them last-minute advice and told them to be good, and then headed on back. Whatever was wrong with the motor was only getting worse. To keep from thinking fearful thoughts I began singing hymns and praising God at the top of my voice, thanking Jesus for protection and exalting the Lord's name in every manner I could think, trying to drown the noise of the banging motor with my voice. I refused to harbor any negative thought. With every jolt and sputter, I just kept verbalizing my prayers of thanks louder and louder.

That was a long nine kilometers. When I finally reached home and rounded the curve in front of the house, the convulsing motor was making so much noise, I could hardly hear myself singing. Finally with an enormous explosion it banged to a stop right in front of our darkened house. I quickly got out of the car and hurried into the house. Why were there no lanterns lit? Why so quiet? Where was everyone? Not a creature was stirring. I called out my litany of *"Vera-Cota-Neny, onde estão?"*—Where are you?

A muffled reply came tentatively, "Mom?"

"Yes! Where is everybody?"

They all began crawling out from under their beds and the closets and the hiding places where they'd scrambled when what sounded like the beginning of the Third World War came roaring up the road. We lamely laughed, and then I recounted how I had felt miraculously transported over those roads in that wretched Jeep. We had a lot to thank Jesus for, I added, as we gathered for our evening prayers.

The next morning when the sun came up and you could see (electricity is a wonderful boon that few appreciate until they've lived without for a season), the young man who was the *fazenda's* driver (and who had shown up with some limp excuse late the night before) came to the door with an awed expression on his face. *"Senhora,* you should never have been able to drive that Jeep back last night. Come look."

I went with him followed by the children who were still shook up and who obviously had been talking about it before I came on the scene. The hood of the Jeep was folded back to reveal the motor—which I knew nothing about so couldn't understand why I was being shown the problem. Then I peered into the motor cavity. Even I could see the difficulty. The battery was dangling by one wire, completely off the battery mount, a few inches above the ground.

What had really happened was that the head gasket had blown—but somehow I managed to get home before the engine froze. Had a guardian angel been holding the whole thing together until I reached the circle in front of the house? Or was the whole transport on wings of eagles? I only know for sure that one more time God was providing me with a sense of being cared for in such a generous manner. And it also was a lesson for the family, who knew God had somehow intervened on our behalf again and we had to praise the Lord for such loving concern.

It was one more stepping stone on the path for us all to learn to trust God. I never had to convince the children that God loved us and provided for us. I wasn't a perfect mother. I'd yell and get impatient and upset with their transgressions, but it was a good life. We had wide open spaces and jungles full of adventures. And we all remained free from the many tropical diseases that seemed to beset others around us. We were even free from most accidents—and the probabilities here were increased enormously by my rambunctious sons, to say nothing of their grandfather.

Ever since he was a young man, my father had had a penchant for putting up incredible swings wherever he went. The jungles only multiplied the possibilities—the 150-foot tall trees in the rain forest out our back door constantly intrigued him. These trees had sprouted in dense forest and then shot straight up in search of the sun before sending out their first branch. Now with clearings on every hand, these high-rise branches were exposed to view—and available.

Papa would start with an arrow and a string and when he'd shot this successfully over the chosen branch, he'd start pulling up heavier and heavier cords until he'd advanced to a weight-bearing strength. Then he'd tie one end of this rope to a mule and drive the mule down the road to pull Zezinho (the smallest and wiriest of our boys) on the other end up the 100-plus feet until he reached the branch. There he would secure the knot to the chosen branch. Zezinho loved being picked by Grandpa for this special task and learned to tie precise knots—knowing full well his future survival depended on them. Then the two connivers would tie a sack stuffed with straw to the bottom to make a seat and voilà—a sack swing was ready for testing.

It took a certain amount of risk to put up those swings, and since I had little trust in either of those two, they never managed to remember to tell me until it was a *fait accompli*. Knowing how much I enjoyed swings, they'd invite me to be among the first to try it out. It was hard to be angry when you were sailing on wide arcs above the jungle floor pulled as high as you dared before you let the placid mule's rope go. If I complained about the danger involved, Papa would get his most innocent look on his face explaining how it was really an educational experience. Among other things this was a wonderful lesson in geometry, for they were learning all about fulcrums and levers and inclined planes. Besides they'd prayed and asked God to protect the enterprise.

There were a few escapades I felt went too far. Like the time Zezão and Graciano used nails and slats to bang a ladder up the side of one of those giant trees. They'd spotted a toucan's nest at the top and wanted to get the fledgling for a pet. I yelled and told them that besides wasting perfectly good boards and nails, risking their limbs and necks, they simply did not know how to raise such a baby bird to maturity. Where was it? Sheepishly they admitted the exposed chick had died.

So we plotted on, the Lord filling my life with good things abundantly while I tended to concentrate on the leaks and garlics I'd left behind. When I complained to the Lord that it seemed a bit unfair that all the other missionaries took two-weeks' vacations, so why couldn't we have an equal opportunity, it felt as though the Lord asked me what specifically was keeping us from a holiday? When I mentioned—for a starter—the cost of transporting, feeding and vacating ten children, I got the sense that the Lord began the "Cattle on the thousand hills" lecture, so I stopped whining and started packing all the kids in and headed to the beach (a 17-hour drive away) for our two weeks.

Finally I figured out a third lesson on generosity: If I should give $500 to someone in need today or spend $500 on something I need (or want) today, this did not mean that tomorrow I would have $500 less. Since the Lord was providing our needs, whether or not I gave this sum away or spent it, nothing changed. It didn't alter how much I would have the following day. The corollary to this strange precept is that should I refuse to spend $500 on something we needed (or wanted) or decline to loan or bequeath $500 to someone else requesting my help today, this did not mean that tomorrow I would have $500 more in the coffers.

Hoarding does not produce wealth for someone trusting the Lord to supply their needs. When God is giving you your sustenance, anything you hoard, as the manna-in-the-wilderness story proves, tends to turn to maggots and begin to stink (Ex 16:19-20). By giving away or spending $500 today I was just passing on the generosity I received from the Lord. When this truism sinks into the core of your being it is the most liberating concept imaginable. God's generosity to you and in turn your generosity to your neighbor are part of the Lord's bounteous plan for the universe.

Of course none of us can live at this place of liberation all the time, but even having glimpses in a glass darkly every now and then is thrilling. As Moses said, "You should be happy to give the poor what they need, because then the Lord will make you successful in everything you do" (Dt 15:10). What a wonderful promise! As this fact seeped into my consciousness my life blossomed: by being generous with others until I knew it was going to hurt and by not counting the cost, the Lord was willing to make me successful in whatever I undertook.

We never had enough money to afford to do any of the things we did, but that non-hoarding principle worked, so we always managed somehow. From then on I stopped trying to live within my means and only tried to live in communication with the Lord so that whatever I did would be under God's watchkeeping and protection. On this principle I continue to travel around the world—not financing my trips out of savings or surplus funds, but on the confidence that the Lord who has brought me thus far will continue to provide my needs, my desires and my adventures. Fiscal responsibility is not taught in the wilderness experiences of life. Spendthrift faith is what God calls us to.

And so it was that I learned to live lavishly, reflecting God's munificent treatment with my children. It took a little organizing, but with each passing year, the children grew, got more capable, and my burden got lighter. And my nerve increased in direct proportion. The longest familial adventure was a three-week, 6,000-kilometer camping trip that took us north across a hypotenuse that went through Belo Horizonte and Ouro Preto (Brazil's first capital) up to Salvador de Bahia and then south down the coast to Rio and São Paulo before heading west to our home on the Paraguay border in the southern state of Paraná.

By now my more competent children were also occupying more space, so it required a van and a car pulling a pop-up trailer to transport us and our gear. I had it all worked out on a job chart. Everybody had a number. Every day your number was assigned a different job, so if everybody was functioning on schedule, it worked smoothly and you didn't get bored from having to do the same chore over and over. Severiano, my insouciant 20-year-old son, began calling me *Dona Funçiona* because I'd come into the campsite and find everyone lollygagging around and call out, *"funçiona, gente!"* (function, troops!).

The days were filled with beaches and swimming and exploits. In Bahia the local kids made money selling pop and hammocks and chilled green coconuts (you stick a straw in the top and drink its refreshing, slightly sweetened juice). Severiano thought it was silly to pay for what was growing all around us, so one day he watched the lads at the beach scurry up the coconut palms that grew along the waterfront (all tilted inland by the prevailing sea breeze). His subsequent scraped arms and legs and his sheepish grin were mute testimony to the skill and strength required to make a "U" out of your body, walking up on well-calloused feet and balancing yourself only with your hands while keeping the rest of you away from the jagged palm trunk until you reached the top and those succulent green coconuts.

Aside from George, who compared the trip to beating your head against a wall ("It feels good to stop"), everyone had a marvelous time. Several of my children, now grown, have repeatedly told me how this Bahian escapade was one of the highlights of their life. Four of the older eight were by now living off the farm and two would be leaving when vacation ended. Soon there would be less reason to stay on the *fazenda*. We all knew our life together was winding down, still it was a worthy celebration of our time together, forging family in an impossible situation, living eleven of those years without electricity, learning myriad lessons about surviving in the face of difficulties and hardships and discovering the important truth that we have a generous and gracious God who is truly worthy of our trust.

Through all this I realized that the God who gilds the lily is so much more indulgent of me than I am of myself. I've come to believe the Lord models for us generous behavior hoping we will go and do likewise. I learned a cornerstone lesson on my first trip to Europe. I had gotten involved with the C.S. Lewis Collection at my alma mater when the curator had bemoaned the fact that although they had a wealth of material, much of it was hard to read in longhand and slow going for the researcher. Since I'm a fast typist I volunteered to transcribe a few letters for the Collection to make it easier for scholars to access these letters. A thousand pages and many months later, I found myself in Oxford.

It was there I had an important lesson in freeing myself of hoarding, learning to trust God's generosity. It was 1971 and I had long dreamed of going to Europe. We had $2,000 in our savings and common sense told me to save this fund for a rainy day. But in the midst of complaining to the Lord about never having been to Europe, it seemed as though God was challenging me to use my umbrella fund and go. It was awfully profligate, but in a weak/strong moment I bought my ticket, made my plans and took off to meet up with the curator of the Lewis Collection in Oxford—the first stop on my journey. I justified the whole trip with a six-week itinerary that combined publishing business with pleasure.

Even Dr. K., the curator, was impressed with the serendipity of that trip. Every door opened to me, every contact produced "stuff" for the Collection. I thought it was normative, but Dr. K. kept telling me that he, who went to England every summer pursuing items for the Collection, got into places he'd never been privy to before because rare opportunities kept being offered me. He was quizzical about what all this meant and I admitted I had prayed fervently that the Lord would expedite the trip and make the necessary connections. Strangely enough, in the middle of all this, every day I found a penny. We could be walking across the commons and I would stoop down and pluck a penny out of the grass. Or we would board a double-decker bus and the driver would roar off, lurching me into a seat—on top of a penny. After a few days of this Dr. K. even began to joke about it and when we'd meet he'd enquire, "Have you found your penny yet today?"

Since I have never been known for my good eyesight—having worn glasses since I was a teen—it did seem a bit out of character. But the pennies continued. After a glorious walking tour in the Lake District with a fascinating medley of folk, I went on to Norway to visit my cousins and see the homestead where my father's family came from. Still the pennies continued—on the wharf of Bergen, the station in Oslo. Of course they were now Norwegian öre, but it was their penny equivalent. Day in, day out; country in, country out. What was the story? Was the Lord trying to say something to me? This had never happened to me before in my life. If these were pennies from heaven, why not something worthwhile like a hundred-dollar bill? What could a penny possibly add to my trip? I didn't know, but I did keep all those "found" coins in a separate purse.

Having read the travel guides, I decided that since several of the appointments I had made on the Continent dealing with publishing matters were off the beaten track, the best thing to do would be to rent a small car for at least part of the time. Amsterdam had a large advertising campaign going for their rental cars. The lure was a promise of no drop-off fees any place in Europe. Start your trip in Holland, rent a car and travel where you will, leaving it at your airport of choice. So after Norway I headed for Amsterdam planning to continue my journey through Germany, Switzerland, France and Spain, dropping my rental car off in Portugal from where I was to fly back to Brazil.

I made my reservation, found the car rental agency, filled out the form and was told that there was a $200 fee for dropping the car off in Lisbon. In the view of the Dutch, Portugal was outside the pale of Europe. They wanted a tenth of my trip budget just to leave the car in Lisbon—which any map would show you is firmly in Europe. I felt cheated. I remonstrated, but to no avail. I walked out of the agency refusing to pay their unjust fee, frustrated, furious, tears streaking my face. It was a gray, overcast day and I walked along a canal filled with dirty, murky water, wondering why everyone rhapsodized about clean Amsterdam—it looked totally grubby to me. I was upset with everything and everybody and was trying to figure out what to do next.

Then it seemed as if the Lord were saying to me, "If I can rain down pennies on your stubborn head, can't you trust me for the dollars?" I paused and considered: Do you suppose that's what the pennies were all about? Just because the Lord knew my tendency to worry about money and scrimp unnecessarily? So I turned around and ate humble pie and rented the car.

Even paying the $200 surcharge, I came out ahead monetarily because food and lodging in small towns off the beaten path where I could drive were considerably cheaper than in big city hotels. Besides, it was glorious driving that lovely countryside, meandering through medieval lanes, stumbling on one adventure after another. Always I felt that the Lord was generously providing and protecting me along that route.

Never again, on that entire trip, did I find another pfennig, another centimo, another cent. They stopped, never to start again until months later when I began once more to worry about money. Then it turned into almost a private reminder from the Lord. I would begin fretting about money and would pray and ask the Lord to show me whether or not I was to do something, launch out on another project, go someplace. Instead of the hundreds or the thousands I would need for the new project, there it would be—a penny or a centavo or a small coin, luring me into another adventure with my generous God. Once I had committed myself and started on the endeavor, as the bills came due, the funds would always appear—manna-like—to keep my accounts current, but never enough for a cushion, never a discretionary fund, never a slush reserve. Give us *this* day our *daily* bread.

Once, shortly after moving back to the States with the two youngest, I was contemplating putting them in a private school because they were being treated so horribly at the local Christian grammar school where they were in the sixth and seventh grades. It's a hard age to be in transition, but I had no idea what they were subjected to until one of my fellow seminarians substituted at their school. That afternoon she came over to tell me that if those were her two daughters she would have taken them out of that school yesterday.

I was horrified to hear that in spite of their getting top grades, or maybe because of it, they were being ostracized and teased for not having faddish clothes and for my driving a beat-up old station wagon which had been given to me by a relative when I first arrived. I was disconsolate until another friend suggested a secular girls' school in town.

When I took the two to visit this school, it was love at first sight— both ways. The school was interested in having two such sweet, bright girls in their midst who were tri-lingual and cross-cultural. My girls were delighted at their visit and kept commenting on how everyone they met had said "hi" and smiled at them. I was heartbroken. How could a smile be that noteworthy? How could I not have known what kind of purgatory this so-called Christian school had been for them? When I had telephoned their teacher to ask her about the rejection they were experiencing, she had acted as if I was interfering in her classroom—after all they were getting good grades. What more did I want?

Christian behavior, for a start, but she had no ears to hear my complaints.

Though it was a wonderful match, there was a large financial quandary. For starters the new school wanted a $100 deposit to hold their places for the next year, but this paled as nothing when compared to the tuition fee for the year—$5,000 each—with no scholarship available until the second year. It was about what my whole annual budget had been for our first year in the States—including our tuition bills.

In spite of being grossly exorbitant for our budget, it met all my criteria for being prayable: good education, loving atmosphere, wonderful opportunity. But when I went to pray about this one, I said to the Lord, "Okay. Pennies were fine for these smaller ventures in faith, but this is horrifyingly expensive. I don't think I can afford it, but you have promised to give us our hearts' desires. Our hearts are all set on this, and so we are going to trust you for this new tuition."

Then I added the addendum: "Listen, I don't want to lose that $100 deposit, so if you are going to provide the $10,000 I need to get these girls through this next year, would you please give me a more significant sign than just a penny?"

I laughed the next time I went outside—we were living in a seminary complex of 91 apartments with constant foot traffic of a couple hundred people going back and forth to school—to find staring up at me from the sidewalk a bright, shiny dime. At least it was significantly larger than a penny. Ten times larger, in fact. So I sent in the $100 deposit and the Lord miraculously sent me a check for $10,000 which covered their fee.

A couple weeks later we moved out of the seminary digs and the relative who'd given me the station wagon was helping us move. She was with me when I went back to pick up my mail. I exclaimed to her, "Whoa! Look at this," showing her the check.

She was amazed and said, "Where did you ever get a thousand dollars?"

I said, "Look again."

It was so preposterous for me to be handling such a huge sum that she couldn't even read the zeroes. Even though it was overwhelming, I was not totally shocked. The Lord promises to be a lot more generous with us than we can ask or think, so when we needed it I had finally received a settlement on a project I had done in Brazil that I had assumed would never be paid—but it was, and with perfect timing.

Since that first penny incident in Amsterdam, it has been ever such. I have asked for ludicrous funding—and gotten it. After that first year the girls qualified for scholarships through junior high and high school and on through the best colleges in this country so I never again needed such a large miracle—and never got it. Funding would appear, but in more modest sums because our needs were more nominal.

I had just married Albert when Heather, finishing high school, decided she wanted to go to Georgetown University. When I told him she was applying there, he solemnly lectured me on the fact that we simply could not afford a school of that caliber.

We had been good friends for several years, but he still didn't have the picture about how I operated financially. When I told him that I had always lived beyond my means, so why start worrying about it now, he shrugged in frustration and walked out the back door.

I yelled after him, "Besides, when I prayed about it, I found a penny immediately."

He turned back and gave me a wan smile, but I knew he wasn't convinced even though he'd heard my penny tale. However, five years later when Heather had graduated from Georgetown and Heidi had graduated from Bryn Mawr College, Albert agreed: God is much more will-

ing to be generous with us than we are willing to be generous with ourselves or our neighbors.

Because of my learning to walk with God on matters financial,
added to all my interaction with people who live outside the monied
economies, I know that I have developed fiscal ideas that seem outrageous to those who want to believe capitalism is next to godliness.

One summer I genuinely shocked Albert when my daughters
Heather and Heidi were preparing to go back to college after being
home during their vacation working to earn their spending money
for the next school year. One had gotten a better paying job than the
other so she had $2200 saved while the other had $1800. At the dinner
table on the eve of their departure, I made the pronouncement that I
thought they should split their money and each take $2000 back to
school.

Albert, who had been party to the morning squabbles over sharing
hair ribbons and belts when they were finishing high school (where
they wore uniforms so only the accessories were fightables), couldn't
believe how unquestioningly the two acquiesced to my suggestion.

Later in private when he asked me to explain my motives, I realized
how un-American such sharing might appear. The three of us had
been a tight community for so many years, it didn't seem scandalous
to me at all. They were both facing roughly the same needs at school. I
would have to supplement whatever their earnings didn't cover, so
why not help one another? They had received plenty of assistance
from me over the years; now it was time for them to learn to do the
same.

I had come to believe a basic cause of familial dissension in Western
society derived from unnecessary rivalries fostered among siblings.
Children raised to share equally in a home, eating the same food, enjoying the same junkets, having the same head start, because of differences in personality, intelligence and ability find one of their number
outstripping the others, one becoming a scapegoat, one an under-
achiever, another besting all odds. Instead of helping one another stay

at par with the familial norm, since from their earliest days these siblings had learned to compete, they now start to harass, goad, vaunt or gloat about their differences.

As Christians we cannot buy into this syndrome. We need to reach out with a helping, generous hand to those in our family, in our village, in our world who need help. God doesn't love me more because I can type faster, earn more money, work longer hours than my neighbor. My abilities and motor skills are gifts. I can use them to glorify God, bless my community or simply for my own self-centered desires. It's my choice, but God requires us to answer for how we've dispensed with the earnings from the talents entrusted.

Since in our culture the determining merit badge is the bottom line, I have watched money and success tear apart an inordinate number of families in my community. A family member might be on the verge of bankruptcy, losing a home, or unable to finish schooling, but rather than help the relative out with something concrete, they are given lectures on fiscal responsibility.

I have been amazed to listen to Christians justify why they don't have to answer the question Scriptures ask: "If anyone has material possessions and sees his brother in need but has no pity on him, how can the love of God be in him?" (1 Jn 3:17).

Having observed heirs engage in mortal combat for a few thousand dollars, preferring to destroy any semblance of family in order to get more "stuff" or what they consider as a fair share of the family treasure, I decided this materialistic foundation to our culture was destructive and un-Christlike. I had no interest in driving a wedge between my two daughters by allowing the one who was luckier to get the better pay go back to school feeling superior, richer or better off. As long as I had anything to do with it, they were going to be encouraged to share and give to those in need. Thus I urged them, in recognition of all the generous ways they'd been treated by God and everyone in their world, to turn around and be generous to one another—and to their neighbors as well.

Of course I have lessons to learn from them, as well. Once after she'd graduated and didn't have all that much money one of my daughters loaned $1,000 of her earnings to a new boyfriend of whom I was deeply suspicious. When he failed to repay her—and vanished in the process—I started to chide her about this poor loan.

She drew herself up and said, "I think it was a cheap bargain. I knew he had a problem with money and I wanted to believe that he had reformed. But if it only cost me $1,000 to learn he was a charlatan, I don't feel badly. Think how many women have spent years and lost a fortune over men who were a lot worse than Jeff?"

From the mouth of babes. . . . Here I was, judging by the bottom line again and she clarified it simply. If he wanted to cheat her, better to find out while they were just dating rather than get serious about someone who was not going to be trustworthy. Besides, it was Gospel living. I'd been the one who had lectured them about giving to those in need around them. Just because I didn't like the recipient, didn't mean she wasn't living the Gospel.

We are to give to those who ask and let God take care of the payback.

Which brings us to an eighth principle of prayer: *You reap what you sow. By being generous and gracious to those around you who are in need, you can expect God to be generous to you when you come to the Lord with your prayers and requests and desires.*

You can't outgive the Lord, an old missionary told me, and I found this to be true. No matter what I gave away to those in need, I never lacked because of it. I learned the truth of the Scriptures which say, "Don't worry about anything, but pray about everything. With thankful hearts offer up your prayers and requests to God" (Ph 4:6). The Bible is full of wonderful promises to those who are generous—I guess God knows we need all the encouragement we can get in this regard.

But on my own pilgrimage, every step of the way, God has been more than generous with me—heaped down, running over generous.

In the process I've learned a little about being generous with others. Throughout my life I have found that incredible blessings come to those who give, but learning to be generous to the unworthy, the ungrateful and the unrepentant is too Christ-like for our justice-calibrated sensibilities. It is here, however, where our prayer life can help us finish a little of Christ's work on earth.

PRAYER FOR GOD'S BENEFICENCE

Lord of all power and might, the author and giver of all good things: We see on every hand examples of your gracious generosity to us; graft in our hearts the love of your Name so that we might show pity to those in need; increase in us true religion so that we may encourage and help our neighbors; nourish us with all goodness and make us instruments of your peace; and bring forth in us the love of God and the fruit of good works; through Jesus Christ our Lord, who lives and reigns with you and the Holy Spirit, one God for ever and ever. Amen.

9.

On Listening

"What are you doing here, Elijah?"

(1 K 19:13)

Prayer is part of a communication system with God. Just as listening is an important element of any conversation with another person, so learning to discern what God is saying to us through the signs of our life is crucial to our walk with God.

If you spend much time contemplating the stories told in Scripture you come to the realization that most of God's actions are unpredictable—blows from behind, if not jabs below the belt.

But how can we possibly understand what is on the Mind who created dinosaurs and mosquitoes? Since we are pretty much in the middle of the food chain, our perspective is limited, but still our souls long for the Lord and our spirits rejoice in God our savior, as Mary's Song recounts (Lk 1:45-47). The real significance of Mary's declaration is that she tells us that God's "mercy extends to those who fear the Lord" (v. 50). For some reason we have been chosen, lifted out of the food chain and gifted with free choice, so that we might stand before our God with fear and trembling, working out our salvation. With this boon of free choice we can go on to the heights of sainthood, the depths of depravity or the steppes of mediocrity. But we are called to be saints, and saints are noted for their ability to hear what God is trying to say to them through their personal history.

Elijah's story is typical. After standing up to the wicked priests of Baal against all odds, bringing the fire of God down to prove to the people that the "Lord is God" (1 K 18:39), Elijah flees into the desert to escape Jezebel's murderous threat. In the wilderness he is miraculously fed by angels but is despondent. When God asks what the problem is, he replies, "I have been very zealous for the Lord God Almighty. The Israelites have rejected your covenant, broken down your altars, and put your prophets to death with the sword. I am the only one left and now they are trying to kill me too" (19:10).

It would seem pretty self-evident that a little sympathy would be in order, but instead God says, "Go out and stand on the mountain in the presence of the Lord, for the Lord is about to pass by."

Then comes the hard-to-understand part: "A great and powerful wind tore the mountains apart and shattered the rocks before the Lord, but the Lord was not in the wind. After the wind there was an earthquake, but the Lord was not in the earthquake. After the earthquake came a fire, but the Lord was not in the fire. And after the fire came a gentle whisper. When Elijah heard it, he pulled his cloak over his face and went out and stood at the mouth of the cave" (v. 11-13).

In the midst of all that pandemonium—what in common parlance we call "acts of God"—how did Elijah discern the voice of the Lord in the gentle whisper? It's a mystery, but the more you walk with the Lord, the more you can hear the voice of God when it whispers in your ear. A crucial factor in hearing God is learning to see the signs. As the wag said: "Good judgment comes from experience and experience, . . . well, that comes from bad judgment." If you reflect on the happenings in your life, especially the times you take pratfalls, you can often perceive that the Lord was trying to keep you from what-have-you by slamming the door in your face—but you insisted, shoving and pushing and clamoring for entrance until you charged the gate and proceeded to land on your nose.

The basics of listening are easy to discuss, harder to practice. No one I know who has what appears to be a meaningful relationship with God has achieved this without a disciplined life of prayer, Scripture reading and reflection. This means a daily linkup—a constant acknowledgement that God's presence surrounds you. The community of faith can also be a powerful support system in your walk with God to keep you from stumbling on the rocks along the pathway as well as a source of strength that hauls you out of the ditch (or as John Bunyan called it, the "Slough of Despond") and dusts you off for the next section of your journey. Surrounding yourself with God's people also precludes your getting away with wailing, like Elijah, "I, even I only, am left" because you soon realize how many others are also ardently wanting to establish a prayerful relationship with their God.

Of course the community of believers (or disbelievers, as is sometimes the case) can be a debilitating force as well. Usually a good clue is to observe how you feel about yourself for having been with this group: Is your self-confidence increased so that you feel buoyed by the group and challenged to higher ground? Or do you, instead, feel incapable of pleasing God without the approbation of the group? The latter is a warning signal. No one, in my estimation, should broker your relationship to the Lord.

Having determined to establish a relationship with your God, there are some postulates that can help keep you on track. One that has saved me a lot of grief is the axiom that God is not the author of confusion. Whenever I am in turmoil, I have found it behooves me to stop and listen. Move ahead only when you have a sense of peace. Out of that quiet center you can proceed, secured and protected from any gale-force winds that might blow your way. If things get jumbled and you need to rush frantically here and there in order to pull off your project, it probably means God hasn't choreographed this one. Get calm, ask for guidance and then listen for the gentle whisper that no storm or tornado can drown out.

This axiom doesn't work only when you are forging grand policy statements, life goals and future aspirations. It is great for car pooling, party giving, vacation planning and any other prosaic aspect of your daily life. The first step in listening to the Lord is trusting that God is in every moment of your life. So when the car pool doesn't work out as hoped, if you insist and push ahead, you're apt as not to find that the kid you kept trying to force into the pool was coming down with strep throat so now everyone riding in the car is contaminated. God was just trying to save you a lot of aggravation, but you were too busy to listen. Once you posit that the God of every moment is worthy of your trust, you can relax. Pray about it. Ask the Lord to show you what you're supposed to do in this situation.

I learned this lesson in Brazil where the vexations of life were constant. Aside from a corrupt political system, inadequate services and a criminal military establishment, everything else was fine. Time and again, rather than fight this system in my own might, I let God go to battle for me. Getting a driver's license, a marriage license or even a birth certificate is a totally corrupt process. Most people at the bottom of society wait until election year and then a politician, in exchange for the promise of a vote, will cut the necessary red tape and hand them what they are petitioning. People at the top of society have connections and so have no such need—the red tape is cut by their friends, or their in-laws' friends, or their godparents' friends. A foreigner who has no vote and no connections appears to have no access to licenses, certificates or power.

You might think I'm being harsh, but this year we were back in Brazil when an international consortium of business and governmental leaders around the world rated countries on their "transparency" which is the code term now for how much corruption is endemic to the system. Brazil was fourth from the worst (New Zealand was the best).

Everyone I knew just shrugged and said, "Yep, there's a lot of corruption here." I would exclaim, "Do you know what kind of revolution would happen in the States if we got rated that poorly on such a list? We'd throw out the entire government and start over!" But such an upset presupposes that someone decent, honorable and upright would want to work in government, and in Brazil that's not likely to happen before the millennium.

After my being in the jungle for five years with no Brazilian driver's license, it started to get problematic. I never got stopped, but the stories began to be told of a new police presence in the area. First a watermelon or some small token of appeasement to the cop would suffice whenever a traffic roadblock might stop one of our American community—the officials were mostly looking for stolen vehicles on their way to Paraguay (which was silly, because everyone knew the police were the ringleaders of these car-theft mobs), but they put up a good front. Then the police started to get greedier, so various Americans decided to face the music and get a license.

When we joined the throng, I was outraged after the receptionist at the county seat explained that the best procedure was to pay $285 to an "expediter" (who handled the proper bribes to the proper sources and took a proper cut for these efforts) because it was virtually impossible for a layperson to get through the labyrinth and handle all the necessary paperwork without such help. My hackles went up and I said absolutely not. I didn't need one because in those days I hardly ever drove off the *fazenda* and it was too scandalous a price.

To make a long story short, I prayed about it over lunch and then told the Lord that if I was to have a license, please work it out miraculously that day without all the endemic bribery. When offices opened up again in the afternoon I went to the principal station determined to figure out the system and do it myself. To get the first signature I had to wait for the clerk, who apparently needed more than two hours to complete his lunch.

Suddenly the army major in charge of our whole district (it was still a frontier area under military rule in those days) strode in, checked out the mendicants standing around the room and then came over. He asked me what I wanted, and I said I wasn't waiting to see him—only the clerk to get a signature for a driver's license. He said that would be no problem. He would be glad to handle that and invited us into his office. I started to protest, but it did seem as though this was a miraculous answer to my prayer. Somehow the major had heard about the kids and told us he wanted to show us the orphanage he had helped start in this little town of Cruzeiro, so if we would just sit down, as soon as his sergeant was free, he'd have him handle the necessary paper work for us.

Later I was told his nickname was *Major Bolinhos* (Major Little-Pills) because he ran the largest drug ring in our state and was probably a drug addict himself—and probably high when he walked in that afternoon. But I was too naïve to suspect anything, so I was duly impressed as he escorted us around their establishment and asked endless questions about the States and what we were doing in Brazil.

I kept looking at my watch and he kept assuring me his sergeant was handling everything and not to worry. Finally at four when all the offices were closing for the day, he told the sergeant to escort us to all the offices, making them all open up especially so the photographer could take my picture, the doctor give me the eye exam, the mechanic show me an engine (I was supposed to identify every moving part! Ha! We smiled at each other lamely and he nodded me on to the next section) and the agent give me a driver's test.

It was an incredible power play. The major wanted to show me how they all would dutifully sign, stamp and deliver—after hours—the most professional license you can get in Brazil, which allows me to drive anything that moves for the rest of my born days (with an occasional eye exam which I have never renewed). All for free—and no vote, either. Then he invited us home for afternoon coffee so we could meet his wife and children before setting off on the three-hour drive home having eaten something.

And you expect me not to believe in miracles?

I do not know why God puts up with all that corruption—and then got me my license without having to bribe anyone. Neither can I understand why I had to go through all those years of abuse—nor why my days of captivity were ended when God led me out of that marriage in a most providential manner and then provided miraculously and bountifully over the next years as I set up housekeeping as a single mother putting my two youngsters through school while I went to seminary and got a master's degree. Nor can I, who always believed that divorce was the worst sin and remarriage just compounded this, explain why God let me meet in a most fortuitous way a splendid and trustworthy Christian (truly a gentle man) with whom I have forged a delightful marriage the second time around.

I admit I learned enormously from my failure. I never intended to have a botched marriage and it seemed incredible, after all the good deeds I had racked up, that someone, somewhere, wasn't going to show up to fix my first marriage. But no fairy godmother appeared and I had to bear the stigma of being divorced in a world where that wasn't acceptable. Humiliation is hard for me and I'd arduously resisted being humbled. The epistle to the Philippians tells us that in Christ's life humility was directly linked to obedience. Jesus—the way, the truth and the life in whom the Father was well-pleased—still managed to "humble himself and become obedient" (2:8).

Now I know that in clinging to my pride, I condemned myself to this suffering. At the time, all I knew was that God was my sole support system. To this day I marvel at the miraculous, split-second choreography that propelled me out of Brazil.

My family and most of the missionary community did not champion my cause—nor even want to know why I was leaving. The only exceptions were my Brazilian friends and Jackie and Dick, missionaries who had been living on the *fazenda* for over a year and had seen at close hand George's choler. My pride never allowed me to talk about the abuse and the unfaithfulness until just before I left. When the news got out, a missionary couple came hurrying over to ask what my justification as a Christian could possibly be for doing what I was doing. When I started telling them I could no longer live with the violence, they changed the subject and went home. Everywhere I turned I got the message that no one wanted to know why I was venturing to leave; they were merely threatened by my decision to challenge authority. Living a lie was preferable to upsetting the status quo.

I thought that many in the missionary community in our vicinity were my friends, for I had hosted a multitude of events. They all liked coming to the *fazenda* because of the horses, the kids, the swings, the activities. But I found that no one cared enough to ask for the reasons I felt I must leave. On the contrary, those who didn't try to cheat me (by non-payment of sums owed to me) tried to connive with George to kidnap my two youngest so I couldn't take them back to the States. At this point the Lord stepped in. I'd found God wasn't willing to annihilate George, but neither was the Lord going to allow them to get away with such a contemptible deed. With breathtaking choreography God intervened at the last minute.

I'd been threatening to leave for years, but one violent act added the last straw. Something inside me snapped. I knew it was wrong to raise my children in this kind of violence. Instead of asking God to solve my problems by disappearing my tormentor, I stopped acting the victim and instead asked God to help me leave. The speed with which it all happened made it seem as though God said, "What took you so long?"

You cannot make rules for our creative God.

Heather and Heidi had just lost a year of schooling. Vera, who had administered their correspondence classes, had exhausted her saintly patience with them and announced she was quitting after the fifth grade. She claimed her English and science weren't good enough to stay ahead of them, but no one else wanted this thankless task. When George announced he would be responsible for their schooling, I knew him well enough to expect he would not follow through. However, they were a year ahead of their peers and, having always been the youngest in my class in school, I felt there were real problems with that position, so I decided that a lost year wouldn't be all that bad for them.

But now their year of freedom had ended and they needed to get back in school. I knew I didn't have the patience to teach them and I was unwilling to subject them to the boarding school life that I had lived.

The kidnapping plot transpired the day I announced my intentions. I had put off telling anyone, not wanting to deal with another violent attack, but Jackie and Dick were leaving the *fazenda* for an extended furlough. Rather than have them find out two weeks later that I'd scampered north on their heels, I decided to let everyone know I was taking the two youngest to the States for schooling. I did not talk divorce because I couldn't face the thought of actually going through with such a traumatic act, but the time had come to live separately. Jackie and Dick weren't shocked—just saddened. She was teary-eyed as she bid me farewell, knowing full well how painful the path ahead would be for the girls and me and that it could never again be the same for any of us.

I thanked her for her concern and then asked if she'd do me a favor. Jackie and Dick were spending the weekend before leaving the country at a mission home in Umuarama so they could say good-bye to all their friends and church associates there. In the 15-year interval since we first landed on that dirt runway in Umuarama, the town had mushroomed from the few blocks of shops with planks for boardwalks only in front of the more prosperous establishments until now the streets were paved, and they even had 24-hour electricity and telephones—all the comforts of good living. I asked Jackie if please, as soon as she got to Umuarama, would she call and leave an urgent message for a missionary friend, Rich, who lived on our second farm which was on the main highway that had recently been hooked up to the telephone line. I also told her I'd be in Umuarama later that afternoon to let my Brazilian friends in town know about my plans and get Heather and Heidi's passport pictures taken. We would stop on our way home to say good-bye one more time.

There were three friends to whom I had to tell my story face-to-face. The rest of the town would hear soon enough, but these were close friends and I wanted to explain personally why I was leaving. As one said, among many tears, "I always suspected that you had problems, but I never realized how serious they were."

The conversations were impossible to hurry through, so by the time the girls and I got to Jackie's it was much later than I had anticipated. She greeted my apology with her own saying she was really sorry but she'd forgotten all about calling Rich until after four. Incidentally, did I know that George had gone to our second farm that afternoon?

I said, "No, I don't think so. He was on the *fazenda* when I left and said nothing about going anywhere."

Jackie looked bewildered and then shrugged, "Well, I know he was there because when I called Rich and said I had a message from you, he was looking out his office window as he answered the phone and commented, 'Well, here comes George now.'"

So because of the split-second, perfect timing interval, I found out about the kidnapping scheme the missionary community on our second farm had unanimously agreed to. Had Jackie called a minute later George would have sworn them all to secrecy. Seconds earlier, he would not have been in sight. Since Rich had no suspicions that George's presence was classified information, he was merely mystified why Jackie was calling from Umuarama with a communication from me when I could have sent it with a direct messenger.

That tiny piece of information changed my life and the lives of my daughters irrevocably. George was speechless when I got back to the *fazenda* and asked why he'd gone out to our other farm. He had no idea how I would know, but when he refused to disclose his motives, my stomach clutched. Something was dreadfully wrong here.

As soon as we'd driven in he had uncharacteristically come out to greet us and ask if he could carry in the groceries. This aberrant behavior immediately made me wary. My children used to say I had eyes in the back of my head because I could always tell when something was up. But like most mothers, I merely had my normal grids for sound

and behavior. Anything that did not fall through the routine, accepted grid, tended to motivate me to investigate what was out of synch
here.

Then, while I was making the girls a bite to eat and George was
unloading the car—a job he usually pawned off on the boys—I heard
a muted click out by the car that made me even more suspicious. All my
antennae were up. At that point I knew I had to stop and listen. Something terrible was in the works and God was doing everything possible
to get my attention.

I knew this information about his trip to our second farm had been
given me supernaturally and I needed to heed every signal. Something
also told me not to let these two children out of my sight, so I decided
to sleep in their room that night. With amazement I realized my parents must know what was happening, because as I was tucking the girls
in, George went across the path to talk to them.

By the next morning the plot fell out. When I'd agreed to return to
Brazil, George had promised that should I ever want to leave again,
he'd not only pay for the trip but sign the necessary documents so
there'd be no difficulty taking Heather and Heidi with me (Brazil
being a paternalistic country, everything moves and has its being on
the whims of fathers). But this morning he admitted he'd been lying
all along and had never intended to let the girls go or pay for our trip.
Also, while I was telling my friends good-bye, he had stolen our passports from my desk, closed my bank account and taken all the money.
The noise I'd heard the night before came from his removing the distributor cap from my car in order to "ground" me.

Having lost the surprise element, the conspiracy soon crumbled.
That split-second programming of Jackie's phone call started the
unraveling of the kidnapping plot. In the end George reluctantly
signed the girls' papers. He didn't pay for my trip but he gave back my
own money and put my car back together—all in the name of Christian forbearance. With this obviously supernatural choreography helping me out of Brazil, I could only assume that God cared about me

and my children more than the Lord was concerned with the pieistic rules set by the missionary community and labeled as Christian.

I have no idea why I was liberated from my bondage. Not everyone is relieved of their pain. I know a lot of women have gone to their graves after having endured enormous suffering at the hands of cruel despots. Women in India today are being burned alive so their husbands can keep their dowries but marry someone else. I tend to feel guilty when I read things like: "Most women throughout most history lived in obscurity and died in misery after exhausting themselves in the inexorable struggle to put bread on the table" (*The New York Review of Books*, 8/10/95:22). Why I was blessed with emancipation I have never figured out.

So when do you turn the other cheek and when do you ask the angel of the Lord to open the prison doors? When do we let them throw us to the lions and when do we call down fire and brimstone on the heads of the wicked? The secret to finding answers to such questions is bathing your life in prayer. If you have turned your life and your moments over to God, the tension that might develop between a fatalistic posture and making the leap of faith is resolved by discernment—developing ears to hear the still, small voice—then carrying on boldly in prayer. You do have to be moving in the direction of progress, as my dad used to say, in order to be directed of the Lord. Couch potatoes do not develop into saints. Another pivotal axiom to remember is that just because it might be better if something happened so, does not a prayer consist.

When Albert first proposed to me there seemed to be a lot going for us, but I hesitated because we were from such disparate worlds. He was a nice campus minister from a mainline denomination who had worked for 20 years on the same campus. I was always headed for the horizon and found it hard to think about putting roots down anywhere. Heather and Heidi were about to be un-nested, so I would soon be free to wander. And then there was my prayer life. We were good friends, and he knew prayer was an important part of my life, but I had always been private about my prayer world so I didn't think he knew how far out my prayer friends were.

There was a bit of temerity in my soul when I asked him if he wanted to attend a Friday night prayer meeting at Agne Sanford's house. He paused a brief second and then cheerily agreed to go. I said to the Lord, "This one's in your hands."

I told Edith I was bringing Albert and she said, "Great!"

I knew there was no point in telling Agnes because she was now 82 and her short-term memory was fading rapidly. I explained to Albert how we all accommodated Agnes's lapses and assured him he would be amazed at how powerful her prayer life remained (little knowing the immensely prophetic utterance I had just made).

Agnes immediately took to Albert, her pale blue eyes sparkling at this nice-looking, clean-cut man. After introductions all around, Agnes looked squarely at Albert and asked if he knew what the prayer of faith was all about. He hesitated long enough for her to be convinced he didn't, so she launched into an explanation: first you get your discernment from God about what you should pray for, then you pray for it using positive imagery, and then you thank the Lord, who promises to hear such prayers, for having done what you prayed for.

"Now do you understand?" she asked. He smiled halfheartedly and I could feel his discomfort zone rising. She continued, "So, is there something we could pray about for you tonight, Albert?"

He demurred. Nope. He needed nothing. Everything was fine. Thank you very much.

"Well, we'll come back to you later. Maybe you'll think of something," she responded sweetly.

Only some ten people were in attendance that night, so the requests of the circle were handily despatched. Agnes did them one-at-a-time to facilitate her memory, which was really quite good that evening. And she certainly remembered that Albert was still to be tackled.

That sly fellow was ready for her. Well, yes, there was something. For the past 13 years he had been hoping for an office on campus at the state university where he works, but because of the separation of church and state problems, that had never been possible. A group of campus ministers had banded together a few years before and rented a small house facing the campus to use as an office, but then they had lost that to eminent domain when the university decided they needed to expand their parking lot. Now he was camped on the third floor of a Presbyterian church a couple of miles from the university, but it was difficult to maintain a presence on campus with no permanent site and the fluctuating student population to deal with.

Agnes cheerfully said, "Oh, well that's easy enough!"

My heart sank because I doubted that Agnes was cognizant enough of constitutional law to realize how un-"easy" such a request was. In fact, I thought Albert was playing foul on that one, but I sat back to let the Lord handle it.

Agnes's prayer was wonderful. She not only asked that Albert be given an office on campus to facilitate his ministry, but she expanded the prayer and asked God to give him the wisdom to know how to use that office once he got it.

Why was I surprised when the following Wednesday a rather subdued Albert reported that he had gotten a phone call that day from a vice-president at the university asking him if he'd seen the paper? Apparently the Supreme Court had just handed down a verdict on an appeals case concerning *Campus Crusade vs. Missouri*. This para-church organization had sued the state of Missouri because the public university there provided rental space for flower shops, travel agents, pubs and pizza parlors on campus, but refused to allow religious organizations to have equal access. The Supreme Court ruled in favor of Campus Crusade and now this vice-president was following up on that precedent, calling to ask Albert, as president of the local campus ministry group, if he could put together enough on-site religious workers to occupy a four-office suite that happened to be empty—for free.

He could, and did. He and his colleagues have been on campus ever since, an integral part of the university's life and an available ministry to all who are looking for religious counseling during these strenuous years. And since then, he has never, ever questioned the ability of prayer to do the impossible.

I again marveled at how this woman, with her simple, bedrock faith, could not only hear the still, small voice but could move mountains. How did she know that it would be "easy" to pray for an on-campus office? Who can explain it? Who can tell you why? Fools give you reasons; the wise never try to clarify how you develop ears to hear that gentle whisper in the midst of life's storms. Over the years Agnes had developed a sense of discernment that took her to the heights, and every time you were with her you learned a little more about the prayer of faith.

Agnes had been to the far corners of the prayer world but besides learning a lot from her about prayer the last summer she was alive, I also learned considerable about aging saints and senility. Edith asked me to stay with Agnes while Edith summered at her home in Maine. Edith's main fame in life did not come from making concessions. There was one way to do everything and she held a monopoly on that. Edith knew my girls were going to be in Brazil for the summer and I think also she was convinced she had cowed me enough so I wouldn't question her authority, make waves, or in any way disturb the systems Edith had left in place.

Agnes loved to go to the beach, but her good shoes were not to be worn on these excursions because sand was bad for the leather. Knives, forks and spoons went in the drawer just so, with spoons nesting and knife blades facing the same direction. There were plenty more trivial pursuits. Having a good memory was about my best asset that summer. The object of the game was to keep Agnes on an even keel—occupied with tasks she enjoyed and taking her medicine promptly and properly. Reading was getting a bit difficult now because Agnes often forgot what was on the previous page. The synapses were snapping but that didn't mean she needed to feel bad about her deteriorating state.

Though Agnes was sweetly forgetful, we still had wonderful and memorable talks about her experiences with the Lord—whether in the body or not, she wasn't always sure. When she was on, Agnes could recount wonderful visions of the New Jerusalem. ("Gates of gold" or "streets of shimmering glass like big pearls" did not quite capture what she'd seen, but that was the best imagery the New Testament writers could come up with—she had difficulty herself finding the words. It was the most brilliant, luminous place imaginable with light coming from within everything so there were no shadows. All rather strange, hard to describe really.) Agnes admitted she didn't know whether this was a vision or whether she'd been there in person, only that she was left with this wonderful memory. She had seen a few other places as well, and in fact she could hardly wait to get back.

One day she had a beatific smile on her face as she told me the Lord had said she could come home the next year—but I wasn't to tell Edith because she would be too sad to learn this. By now I had been subjected to so many repetitions of the same story and muddled approaches to various issues that I doubted seriously Agnes had not already told Edith. If not, she would probably do so as soon as Edith got back from Maine. But it certainly wasn't my role to discuss Agnes's revelation with Edith when she got back, so I didn't bring it up.

It was like watching a melodrama unfold that winter—everyone who had been important in Agnes's ministry came through California. Without a word, with no coördination, and certainly no appeal from Edith. They happened to be passing through and stopped to pay their respects to a woman who had always been at the forefront of the healing community and had launched many of them in their own prayer ministries of the church. No one mentioned death or sickness or an imminent departure, but it seemed to me someone was choreographing a huge send-off.

Then in February, a month before blossoms hit any other tree in the vicinity, Agnes's beloved peach trees burst forth in glorious blooms. She was an artist and to be surrounded by beauty was thrilling to her.

The last Tuesday of February, during our usual weekly luncheons, I was astonished to hear myself ask Edith if she had thought about what she would do when Agnes was no longer with us. Instead of being offended by such a probing, personal question—as I would have normally expected—Edith warmed to the topic and we spent the entire lunch talking about her plans for an Agnes-less future. Even though I felt I should be embarrassed about scrutinizing her on such a delicate issue, I felt strangely exhilarated. We parted, planning to meet again Friday night for prayer meeting.

I do not know whence came that prompting to speak out. I just know that often when I've started to say something and get interrupted, I need to stop. If I charge ahead and insist on having my say, it usually turns out I should have kept my mouth shut. So I've learned that when those strange interferences happen, it's best not to push the subject. Other times when I have no inclination to talk about something, I suddenly find myself in a lengthy discussion being led by the Spirit in paths I had no intention of treading.

When I left the pie shop after lunch that Tuesday I still didn't understand the scenario, but it was starting to dawn on me that I was being choreographed for a part in a grand exit finale that was abuilding.

On Friday when we entered Agnes's house, part of me was not surprised to find it felt almost as if I was walking on hallowed ground. There was a hush on the group that had arrived before us. I looked around for signs of anything wrong, but everything looked normal. Then Edith appeared and announced that Agnes seemed to have a touch of the flu and was under the weather. Should we leave? we enquired. No, it would be fine. She just would not be joining us for the prayer group.

We sat gingerly, unconvinced but not wanting to contradict Edith. Uncharacteristically, Edith changed her mind and decided perhaps we had better not stay too long. She then fixed her eyes on me and suggested I pray for Agnes before we leave—her look warning me not to pray anything stupid like asking for a supernatural healing. "Discernment is what it's about!" she silently glowered. So I quieted my soul, asked for guidance and then lifted Agnes to the Lord, asking God to surround her with joy and with her guardian angels who could keep her from stumbling on any rocks along her path.

I felt vindicated when Edith gave me a brusque nod. "That was just right." Edith was never an easy one to hug, but we kissed her good-night and a restrained group walked out into the starry night feeling as if we were surrounded by a company of angels.

The next afternoon I talked to Edith, who reported that Agnes seemed to be somewhat improved. She'd had some orange juice for breakfast, but really didn't want anything else. She'd commented on her lovely peach trees in full blossom but then had gone back to bed. For lunch she'd eaten soup and had a little of her favorite dessert—peppermint ice cream. Edith mentioned that Marge, a member of their church, had volunteered to go to early service the next morning and then stay with Agnes so Edith could attend the eleven o'clock service.

But it was not to be. At eight Edith tried to call Marge to say that Agnes was so much improved that she really didn't feel the need for anyone to stay with her. But Marge had already left for church. By the time Marge arrived, Agnes had had a complete reversal and was already deep into her homeward journey. Just as the clock struck eleven that Sunday morning (when all good Episcopalians prefer to face their Lord) she breathed her last, Marge holding one hand, Edith the other.

It was such an awesome moment that neither could speak. Stunned, they sat wondering what to do. Finally Marge whispered, "Mirror?" so Edith got up and found a little hand mirror which she placed beneath Agnes's nostrils. There was no longer sign of any breath.

Neither ever found adequate words to describe what both agreed was "the most spiritual moment of my life." No sickness. No pain. No sorrow. Just a faithful servant going home for the holidays. Finally the two women went out on the little porch overlooking that lovely valley trying to collect their wits. Suddenly Jimmy, the beloved blue jay who had been absent all winter, came swooping down to stand on the railing as if to say good-bye. He was never seen again. Within the next ten minutes three different people called long-distance to announce, "Agnes is gone, isn't she."

And so a chapter closed. If she had been Catholic instead of Episcopalian, perhaps someone would already be starting the canonization process. But for me it was a wonderful glimpse into the world of learning to communicate with the Lord who has always proven to be worthy of my trust. All these people around Agnes had learned to listen. Listening comes from a quiet core, an open mind, a Christ-centered existence and a purity of spirit. Not perfection—which is beyond the reach of all of us—but a stillness at the center of your being where you are waiting and expecting to hear the gentle voice.

Strangely, when it was all over I finally asked Edith if Agnes had mentioned that the Lord had let her know the year before that she would be coming home now.

No, she had said nothing.

I was surprised. Then I realized that just because she was senile, did not mean Agnes had become stupid; she was just forgetful. It was fascinating to watch the physical body crumble around her saintly soul. And Agnes wasn't perfect. Perhaps a better term for her, rather than calling her a saint, would be to say she was a faithful servant, gifted by the Lord for God's service and willing to share these gifts widely.

Edith was the Martha of our group. I loved this difficult woman deeply, but like Martha she was "troubled by many things" when she could have been quietly sitting at the feet of Jesus, listening to the words of eternal life. Still, I sat by her side for many hours a few years later as she herself died a lingering death, stubborn and bossy to the end.

After Agnes's death, I had prayed, asking the Lord to reward Edith and give her something really special for her faithful service to Agnes in her old age. That summer when Edith was back in Maine, an old neighbor who was a powerful industrialist asked her if she and a friend would care to accompany him around the world. It seemed his private jet would be stopping in Los Angeles that fall and there were a couple of free slots on his 747—outfitted to take twenty-some people in overstuffed easy chairs and the lap of luxury. Of course Peter, the industrialist, had an exclusive bedroom and office suite on board, but it was an impressive setup no matter where you were seated. Edith came back to California with a sparkle in her eye. You knew she was pleased with the prospect of circumnavigating the world.

I was the designated driver assigned to take Edith and her friend to an outlying airport in the Los Angeles basin which handles noncommercial planes. On arrival we found the plane's departure was going to be slightly delayed because Peter was off wheeling and dealing—and the party moved at his whim. Would I mind dropping Peter's son, an oncologist from New York, and his grandson, who was Heidi's age and a junior at a very preppie Eastern school, at a local restaurant where Peter was meeting with his business cronies?

They hopped into my humble Honda (I'd finally asked the Lord for a new car during one of those gas crises we had here in California which made my gas-guzzling station wagon a true liability—and there it came, an unexpected check for $3,000 which got me a nice little car that—compared to the wagon—virtually ran on fumes). Peter's grandson proceeded to ask me how far it was to San Francisco implying he would prefer to have supper there, trying to figure out if I would offer to drive them at least one-way. Instead I dropped them at the nearby restaurant and went on my way, thinking he might be inheriting a huge fortune, but that for all his expensive schooling he had a lousy grasp of American geography.

Edith hated to have me talk politics. She felt that as Christians, all we needed to do was pray and leave the rest in God's hands. Whenever I published articles speaking favorably on what the liberation theologians were doing in Latin America, she harrumphed. At that time Peter the industrialist was then heading up a high-profile commission trying to reduce government waste—read this as: "reduce the taxes on the wealthy and stop spending anything on the poor." If ever I began to remark on the meanness of his effort, I was quickly silenced. Mentioning anything about public policy would make Edith change the subject, cut me off or generally scold—until the summer that Peter's commission got around to recommending that postal service be eliminated from the sparsely populated little island where Edith had her summer home. She came back to California that fall and proudly announced she'd been on TV. It seems there had been a public protest organized and Edith had not only gone, but she'd spoken up (that part wasn't surprising). I made a comment about whose ox was being gored—which she didn't appreciate—but I could never understand how such a devout woman, dedicated to healing the wounds of those she encountered, could turn her back on societal ills.

Though it upset Edith when I asked her to pray for my trips because she thought I was too flighty, she could never tell me she was convinced God did not want me to go and thus refuse to pray. Her prayers always turned out to be soaring invocations commending me to the Lord's service. It was as if her prayer life was on a different plane from her Martha-esque tendencies. In spite of her gruff exterior, she would pray for matters she had no knowledge of, which showed that her spiritual ears were tuned in to the gentle whisper of God's voice.

The bishop who confirmed me when I first returned from Brazil was another who heard the still, small voice and had information from on high. I had been baptized Lutheran by my father, but when it came time to be confirmed I was off in non-Lutheran boarding schools where confirmation classes were not offered. No one seemed to notice I had fallen through the cracks of church membership. After working all those years with my father's Lutheran mission in Brazil, I was ready to jettison all connections with my former life and create my own world.

Years before when I had enrolled in my nice fundamentalist college we were told during orientation week that they expected us to attend church every Sunday—then they handed out a list of approved local churches. They made a point of telling us the Episcopal church in town was not included and they would prefer we not attend there. (Looking back, I suspect it was because they used real wine in the Eucharist service, but at the time I didn't ask and nobody told). With my perverse nature, of course I chose that one as my church of preference. Since attendance wasn't taken, I didn't show up as faithfully as our school administrators prescribed, but I did enjoy the liturgy and serene setting for worshiping the Lord. At the time I also encountered C.S. Lewis' writings and then later Agnes and others I admired who were part of the Anglican confession.

When I returned from Brazil and entered seminary there was a large church across the street that proved to be Episcopalian. The rector was a bit surprised to find out that as a seminarian with a religious background I had somehow avoided being confirmed or joining a church, so I was sent through an adult class for eight weeks.

On the appointed Sunday I showed up for confirmation. I had never laid eyes on Bishop Corrigan—80, long retired and imported from Santa Barbara for the ceremony. Someone did mention he had been a great church leader during his heyday. Among other things, he was one of the three bishops who decided, without benefit of sanctions from their superiors, to stop the debate and just go ahead and ordain women to the priesthood. Jesuits scholars had subsequently studied the case of these eleven women and gave their judgment—theirs was a valid ordination because it met the criteria of having three bishops agree and participate in the ceremony. According to ecclesiastical law they were in the direct line of those ordained to the ministry of Christ.

That Sunday as the various adult confirmands went forward to receive the bishop's blessing I was amazed at how varied and particular were the prayers of this courageous old man of God. Then when I knelt before him, he laid hands on my head and I felt the power stream out of him as he virtually commissioned me to a life of service to the gospel of our Lord, invoking the Holy Spirit's presence in everything I communicated to the world.

After church a friend stopped me to ask, "The bishop had never seen you before, had he?" I shook my head no. "I didn't think so, but that was a remarkable prayer—and so perfect for you!"

I agreed that it had seemed as though Bishop Corrigan had insider information about the entire group. He was hearing things with his spiritual ears that came from a long-term association with the Spirit who intercedes "for us with groanings which cannot be uttered" (Rm 8:26).

When anyone would ask Agnes how you could tell when it was the Spirit's voice, she would say, "You listen to your heart. If it leaps with joy, then you know the Lord is in it. If you are filled with dread or fear, then it's not from the Lord." No wonder she said it would be "easy" to pray for Albert to get an office on campus—she must have immediately gotten the confirmation of the Spirit, and with her experience she knew she was privy to insider information she could work with.

My own children used to ask me, when we were talking about future plans, "But do you really *feel* it is going to happen, or do you just *wish* it would happen?" They knew that when I got the confirmation in my soul about what-have-you, it would happen no matter how preposterous it might appear at that juncture. Just wishing it wasn't good enough.

Listening to the still, small voice also means acknowledging that you do not have all the answers. Nor can you surround yourself with preconceived notions of what God can or cannot do.

Albert has a ministerial buddy who was recently diagnosed with adult-onset diabetes. The last time they were together he didn't look too good, so Albert asked how it was going. His friend explained that he was trying to stay away from drug therapy and solve his health problems with diet—which was proving harder than he had anticipated. When Albert asked if he had tried prayer for healing, his friend—a prominent minister—said he didn't believe in asking God for specific requests. Albert, who has been around too many miracles these past years to buy that one, told him he didn't think God was a generalist.

There just is too much precision in God's creation not to believe that definite requests are okay—especially when you're in pain. I pray about everything—my lost checkbook, parking for a lecture, sickness in the family, tuition scholarships, the health of the nation, the release of political prisoners from unjust captivity. A life of prayer does not guarantee that you will be free of problems, it only assures you will not have to face these alone. The God of the universe surrounds you with love.

We are all clay vessels, cracking and aging, complaining and praising. Listening to the Lord requires being sensitive enough to know when you can let your requests be made known unto the Lord and when the doors are being shut—and then not trying to force them open, accepting that there must be some reasons your way is stymied.

Which brings us to a ninth principle of prayer: *Always be willing to listen to advice. None of us have perfect hearing so it is important to walk humbly with our prayer-answering God who loves to do good things for us.* When you come to the Lord with all your requests—from the most mundane to the most sublime—you can rest assured that the God who loves us more than we can imagine is listening. God will also give us ears that can hear what is being said by the answers we get to these prayer requests. One of the most important aspects of developing a prayer life is learning how to listen.

Strangely enough, when you probe into their personal history of prayer, many people, even agnostics, admit that as children they prayed for something that appeared to be granted them, not because they necessarily "merited" this answer, but simply because they asked. Albert's request as a young boy was to help him find a baseball glove he had dropped on the way home from school. He realized as he was walking along the railroad tracks—where he wasn't supposed to be in the first place—that his glove was missing. The whole way back he pleaded with God to let him find it. A half-mile back when the glove appeared, he thanked the Lord because it certainly seemed like a providential intervention to him—even though he was hardly in a state of grace walking on the tracks he had been expressly forbidden to use as a route home.

Such experiences can either be the foundation for a two-way communication system you set up with God, or you can discount it and rationalize it away, forgetting about it until someone like me comes along and starts to delve into your belief system. I have never understood why so many people I've met who have started out their prayer careers with such positive experiences don't carry on. Usually by the time I meet them they are disconsolate, feeling abandoned by their God, and incapable of believing any good thing will ever be done for them supernaturally.

In our culture it would be like the children of a multimillionaire dying homeless and in rags because they don't want to say please or cash their parent's check or in any way be beholden to the wealth of a parent who is willing to indulge you, care for you and give you adventures beyond your wildest imagination. That's a lot to lose to false pride, in my estimation.

God is willing to take us all on a wonderful adventure of prayer. All we have to do is follow, bow our proud necks, say "please," "thank you," and submit to the God of the universe who has given us so many incredible promises. The psalmist recounts how God dealt with the children of Israel, "You saved them time after time. . . . You answered their prayers when they were in trouble. You kept your agreement and were so merciful." Then the psalmist bids the people, "Let us celebrate and shout in praise of your holy name. Lord God of Israel, you deserve to be praised forever and ever. Let everyone say, 'Amen! Shout praises to the Lord!' " (106:43-48).

None of us can come to God on our own merit or because we deserve this healing or divine intervention. We are all recipients of mercy and grace. Thus it behooves us ever to foster a basic trust in the Lord that undergirds our entire being—all our reactions, all our hopes and dreams. By developing listening ears, we can strive to please the Lord in all that we do and say for the night is coming when no one can work. And at that point we will be asked to make an accounting for how we have spent our days and our hours here on earth.

PRAYER OF TRUST

O God, you have prepared for those who love you such good things as surpass our understanding: Pour into our hearts such love towards you, that, we, loving you in all things and above all things, may obtain your promises which exceed all that we can desire; give us listening ears to hear the gentle voice of the Spirit as it leads us into truth and righteousness; may our trust in your promises grow with each passing moment; through Jesus Christ our Lord, who lives and reigns with you and the Holy Spirit, one God, for ever and ever. Amen.